P9-CPW-421

Thematic Units for Kindergarten

by

Kristin Schlosser

SCHOLASTIC

PROFESSIONAL BOOKS

New York • Toronto • London • Auckland • Sydney

· ·

To Jane Clajus, my first and best teacher, who opened the world when she opened a book

And to all my former and current students at Allison Elementary, who are truly the authors of this book

Scholastic Inc. grants teachers permission to photocopy the reproducible pages from this book for classroom use. No other part of this publication may be reproduced in whole or in part, or stored in a retrieval system, or transmitted in any form or by any means, electronic, mechanical, photocopying, recording, or otherwise, without permission of the publisher. For information regarding permission, write to Scholastic Professional Books, 555 Broadway, New York, NY 10012-3444.

Note: The interactive charts, poems, songs, and fingerplays are works the author has collected over the span of her teaching career. They are either traditional, or original works of the author or of teachers who have shared material with her throughout her career. All attempts to reach and credit the original sources have been made.

Cover design by Vincent Ceci
Cover illustration Susan Pizzo
Interior design by Roberto Dominguez and Jaime Lucero
Interior illustrations by James Hale
ISBN 0-590-49579-8
Copyright ©1994 by Kristin Schlosser. All rights reserved.
12 11 10 9   0 1 2/0
Printed in the U.S.A.

CONTENTS

INTRODUCTION

A kindergarten classroom provides a rich literacy environment in which children are motivated to involve themselves in the reading and writing process. As children discover the enjoyment of reading, they learn its relevance to their individual interests. This creates a literacy cycle: As children develop confidence and competence in the reading process, they increase their motivation and desire to continue reading.

Thematic units are designed to build children's language competence and their knowledge of cognitive structures. Through thematic units, children increase their ability to read and write critically and creatively. Readers apply previous experiences to make sense of new ideas and information. Thus reading becomes a way of bringing meaning to print. Through in-depth study of a theme, the children construct rich multiple representations of the topic.

A thematic unit is an effective teaching strategy for the following reasons:

✔ It invites children to actively participate in a sustained exploration.
✔ It provides children with opportunities to write, speak, listen, and read.
✔ It acts as a catalyst for bringing a wide variety of literature into the classroom.
✔ It enhances literacy skills through meaningful experiences with books.
✔ It provides a context for the development of comprehension.
✔ It aids in building a framework for writing through repeated exposure to narrative structures, patterns, and language.
✔ It meets the individual needs and interests of the children.

The 17 thematic units in this book have been used successfully with kindergarten children. Each theme includes suggestions for group time activities, literature extensions, and thematic book lists. The sections called Area Design show how suggested materials can be used to integrate the theme throughout the classroom.

QUESTIONS AND ANSWERS

How do I choose a theme?

Kid-watching is the best way to choose a theme that will interest young children. Pay close attention to books that seem to spark their interests, topics they tend to write about in their journals, and topics they are eager to discuss. A favorite classroom story could be the springboard to a successful thematic unit. For example, if your children continue to request re-readings of *The Very Hungry Caterpillar*, by Eric Carle, this could be the beginning of a thematic unit about insects or food.

How long should a thematic unit last?

The average theme unit lasts from 2–3 weeks. This depends on the continued interests of your children.

How do I plan for a new thematic unit?

Start with a core of quality children's literature which ties in with your thematic unit. Ask your school or local librarian to help you gather books. Once this collection is in place, read some of the books to the children in your class. This will help you determine if the theme you've chosen will meet the needs and interests of your class.

Would planning a thematic unit with a colleague be helpful?

Yes! Working collaboratively has numerous benefits:

✔ Materials can be shared;
✔ Materials can be created together or divided so that each person contributes something new to the theme;
✔ Ideas can be brainstormed and generated; and
✔ Evaluation of the theme's successes can be discussed, and adjustments made.

Do I have to create all the materials before the theme can be started?

No. A book collection and perhaps one other resource, such as an interactive chart, is a good starting point. This gives the children a chance to contribute to the planning. If you discover that the theme is not meeting the needs or interests of the children then you can reevaluate and restructure without a great loss of time and materials.

Should all the materials in the classroom reflect the theme?

Children continue to revisit, learn, and experiment with familiar materials. Change materials slowly so the children can try new things in a familiar context. This also gives you an opportunity to observe, question, and model new materials that reflect a new theme.

How should I store my thematic materials?

Generally, storing all materials from one theme in some type of box or bag works best. This allows for easy access, set up, and break down. A large bag with handles (available through library supply catalogs), large garbage bags, or cardboard artist-style portfolios are good options. Reproducibles and planning sheets can be stored in manila folders in a filing cabinet. This will allow you to add materials quickly as you discover them throughout the year.

Can I teach strategies and skills using themes?

Reading is taught most effectively within the context of a meaningful whole, allowing children to employ a variety of reading strategies and to construct concepts about the conventions of print. Themes provide an excellent means for children to construct relationships between oral and written language and develop important reading concepts. The Literacy Development section of each theme provides suggestions for effectively guiding children to integrate semantic, syntactic, and graphophonic cueing systems. You can add isolated letter work as the children find it necessary or as your curriculum mandates.

How can I transition smoothly into a new theme?

A mini-theme is useful for this purpose. A mini-theme is a short, concentrated theme lasting a week. It requires fewer materials and time than a full theme unit. Only one or two new resources are added to the classroom for the mini-unit, so the children explore the mini-theme in the context of the materials from the previous unit. This gives the children an opportunity to continue their learning and extend their thinking about the previous theme. A mini-theme also gives you some time to plan and implement the next extensive theme. On the next pages are examples of two mini-themes: The Alphabet and Clothes.

MINI-THEMATIC UNITS

The goals of a mini-unit are to:

- Introduce new literature and reading strategies in a familiar setting;
- Focus on a specific topic for a limited time, usually one to one and a half weeks;
- Provide a transition between extensive thematic units; and
- Allow the teacher to plan and collect for the next theme unit.

The Alphabet

This unit was originally designed as an alphabet review. The children enjoyed the literature and activities so much that I now use this unit at the beginning of December. At that time the children are aware of the alphabet and extend their learning while exploring wonderful literature.

AREA DESIGN

Game Table

- Two grids drawn on paper (divide each paper into 12 squares)
- Basket of plastic alphabet letters
- Spinner or die

Children create their own rules for a game using the above materials. Encourage children to name their game.

Listening Center

Theme-appropriate cassette tape and book: *Chicka Chicka Boom Boom.*

GROUP TIME ACTIVITIES

These activities involve the whole class.

FLANNEL BOARD STORY

- Felt palm tree
- Felt alphabet letter

Children use the materials listed above to retell *Chicka Chicka Boom Boom.*

Literacy Development

✔ Sing the letters of the alphabet to familiar tunes: "I'm a Little Tea Pot," "Twinkle Twinkle Little Star," etc. Allow the children to suggest familiar tunes.

✔ Read *Chicka Chicka Boom Boom.* Distribute individual alphabet letters to children in the class. Dramatize the story and encourage the children to create motions for their letter.

✔ Read *On Market Street.* Cover the words on the bottom of each page and encourage the class to brainstorm different items that begin with that letter of the alphabet. Reread the new version.

✔ Take an alphabet walk. Provide each child with paper and pencil. Walk around the school, stopping periodically for children to record any letters that they observe. Leave the arrangement of the paper up to each child.

✔ Write various letters of the alphabet on self-stick paper. Distribute one letter to each child. The children then find an item in the classroom that begins with that letter and attaches the letter to it. Record their findings.

✔ Read *Where Is Everybody?* Use the pattern of the story to create a new version using the children's names. (Example: Michael is at the Mall, Lindsey is at the Laundromat.)

✔ Create Letter Bags. Each child chooses a plastic bag with a letter of the alphabet written on the front. The child takes the bag home and in it collects items that begin with that letter. After the Letter Bags are returned to school, each child shares his or her contents with the class.

EXTENSION ACTIVITIES

These activities can be used as individual assignments.

✔ *Where Is Everybody?* Pattern Book: Using the pattern of the book, each child draws a self-portrait in a place that begins with the same letter as their name. Bind for a class book.

✔ Class Alphabet Book: Using their Letter Bag, each child chooses one item to illustrate as a representation of that letter. Reproduce and bind as a class book and place a copy in the Writing Center.

✔ *Chicka Chicka Boom Boom* Coconut Trees: Children create coconut trees from construction paper. Use rubber alphabet stamps to stamp letters on the tree. Reproduce the repetitive phrase for each child and encourage him or her to "print" the sentence using the letters on the tree.

MATH ACTIVITIES

✔ First-Letter Graph: Create a graph using the first letter of the children's names. Which letter has the most names?

✔ Individual Alphabet Graphs: Provide each child with a small bag of alphabet-shaped cereal. Children can count the contents and categorize the cereal into rows of the same letter. Which letter is found the most?

COOKING ACTIVITY

✔ Make alphabet soup. Before eating, ask children to say words that start with the letters found in each spoonful.

BOOKLIST

A-B-C-ing by Janet Beller (Crown, 1984)

Alfred's Alphabet Walk by Victoria Chess (Greenwillow, 1979)

Alphabatics by Suse MacDonald (Macmillan, 1986)

Animals A to Z by David McPhail (Scholastic, 1988)

Apples to Zippers by Patricia Ruben (Doubleday, 1976)

Chicka Chicka Boom Boom by Bill Martin Jr. and John Archambault (Simon and Schuster, 1989)

My Name Is Alice by Jane Bayer (Dial, 1984)

On Market Street by Arnold Lobel (Scholastic, 1981)

Teddy Bears ABC by Susanna Gretz (Macmillan, 1986)

Where Is Everybody? by Eve Merriam (Simon and Schuster, 1989)

Babies/ Growing

One year, parents of six children in my classroom were expecting new babies in their home—I was also expecting my first child. This mini "baby boom" became the springboard for this unit. Kindergarten children are fascinated by babies and baby items. I theorize that it allows them to explore familiar materials and routines in a new way along with their own memories of once being babies themselves. This unit continues to be a favorite every year!

AREA DESIGN

Dramatic Play

GENERAL PROPS
- Dolls
- Rocking chair
- Doll beds
- Blankets
- Baby bottles
- Diapers

PROPS TO ENCOURAGE LITERACY
- Books to read to dolls
- Tape recorder and lullaby tape
- Empty baby powder containers
- Cereal

Art Center
- Cotton balls
- Cotton swabs
- Pastel markers
- Pastel paper, tissue, yarn, etc.

Block Center
- Dollhouse
- Doll family

Game Table

- Two grids drawn on pastel paper (each paper divided into 12 squares)
- Basket of baby shower favors
- Spinner or die

Children create their own rules for a game.

Writing Center

- Word cards for baby items: bottle, rattle, diapers, etc.
- Advertisements featuring items for babies
- Blank books made from pastel construction paper

Sensory Table

- Soapy water
- Shape sponges
- Float toys

Listening Center

- Theme-appropriate cassette tape and book, such as a tape of lullabies

Science Center

- Scale and tape measure (for children to weigh and measure themselves)
- Paper and pencil (for recording weight and height)

GROUP TIME ACTIVITIES

These activities involve the whole class.

Oral Language Development

INTERACTIVE CHARTS

The Baby Song

Oh, Mama hurry
Oh, Mama hurry
Oh, Mama hurry
Bring the _____
for the baby.
To stop the crying
To stop the crying
Oh, Mama, hurry
Bring it to the
baby now.

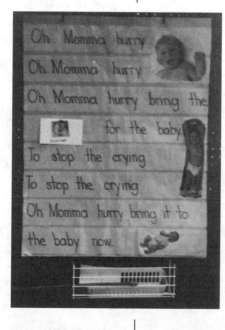

For the blank, create labeled picture cards of baby items: bottle, blanket, pacifier, etc.

I'm Very Happy to Be Me

_____(1)_____ is my hair,
_____(2)_____ are my eyes.
I'm ___(3)___ years old
just the right size.
My name is ___(4)___ and as you see
I'm very happy to be me.

Create a set of name cards and three sets of word cards for the blank spaces in the chart.
1. Blonde/Red/Brown/Black
2. Blue/Green/Brown
3. (child's age)
4. (child's name)

POEMS/SONGS/FINGERPLAYS

One Little Baby

One little baby
rocking in a tree.
Two little babies
splashing in the sea.
Three little babies
banging on the door.
Four little babies
crawling on the floor.
Five little babies
playing hide and seek.
Keep your eyes closed until I say PEEK!

When I Was a Baby

When I was a baby
My family cared for me.
They fed me and they dressed me
And rocked me carefully.
Now that I am older
And go to school each day,
I feed myself and dress myself,
I study and I play.

When I Was a Baby, a Baby, a Baby

When I was a baby, a baby, a baby,
When I was a baby, one, two, three
_____, _____ this way,
_____, _____ that way,
_____, _____ this way.
One, two, three.

Create word cards for the poem. Words might include: goo, goo; cry, cry; crawl, crawl; etc.

FLANNEL BOARD STORY

Create felt pieces to retell the story *Eat Up Gemma!*

Literacy Development

✔ Brainstorm a list of what children know about babies.

✔ Read *Baby's Catalog*. Brainstorm a list of things that babies use. This can be done using a web format, having children classify objects according to a category.

✔ Place assorted baby items in a basket and ask children to match the appropriate word cards to the items.

✔ Read *Jack's Basket* and *The Red Woolen Blanket*. Encourage the class to compare and contrast the two books. Record these comparisons on chart paper.

✔ Allow each child to describe a funny incident that took place when they were babies. Have children discuss what they can do now in comparison to when they were infants. Record their observations.

✔ Read *The Important Book*. List important items about each child in the class.

EXTENSION ACTIVITIES

These activities can be used as individual assignments.

✔ Pastel Paintings: Children can use pastel paints and cotton swabs to create a picture.

✔ Personal Chart of "The Baby Song:" Give each child a photocopy of the interactive chart on page 17. Have children create their own word cards for the blank space.

✔ Guess Who? Language-Experience Book: Ask each child to bring in a baby picture. Photocopy the picture and record each child's words as they recall some memories about themselves as babies. Write the child's name on the bottom of the page and attach a current photo. Cover this with a paper flap. The reader can guess who the story is about.

✔ Baby Collages: Ask each child to create a collage using pictures from baby magazines.

✔ Allow the children to dramatize the actions for "When I Was a Baby" on page 18.

MATH ACTIVITIES

✔ Ask "Do you have a baby in your house?" Graph the responses.

✔ Individual "One Little Baby" Books: Duplicate the poem on page 17. Cut into sentence strips and have the children draw illustrations.

BOOKLIST

101 Things to Do with a Baby by Jan Omerod (Lothrop, 1984)

Baby's Catalogue by Janet Ahlberg and Allan Ahlberg (Little, Brown, 1983)

Eat Up Gemma! by Sarah Hayes (Lothrop, 1988)

Go and Hush the Baby by Betsy C. Byars (Puffin, 1982)

Hush Little Baby by Aliki (Prentice Hall, 1972)

The Important Book by Margaret Wise (Harper Brown, 1949)

Jack's Basket by Alison Catley (Dutton, 1987)

Peek-A-Boo by Janet Ahlberg and Alan Ahlberg (Puffin, 1984)

The Red Woolen Blanket by Bob Graham (Little, Brown, 1988)

Titch by Pat Hutchins (Macmillan, 1971)

Bears

BEARS was the first thematic unit that I used in my kindergarten classroom. I wanted a unit to use at the beginning of the year while the children were adjusting to school. Therefore it had to be familiar, comforting, and exciting. Teddy bears were the perfect solution. The children enjoy bringing their own stuffed bears to school, which became a bridge between the familiar and the unknown. As all teachers know, the variety of bear literature provides an effective way to open the doors of literature and reading for children at this age.

AREA DESIGN

Dramatic Play

House of the Three Bears

GENERAL PROPS
- Housekeeping props: table, chairs, stove, dishes, etc.
- Large, medium, and small bowls and chairs
- Three bears and Goldilocks puppets or dress-up props

PROPS TO ENCOURAGE LITERACY

- Various versions of *The Three Bears*
- Oatmeal boxes
- Recipe for porridge

- Paper and pencils

Art Center

- Bear templates
- Bear stickers
- Various sizes of circle templates to use for creating bears
- Buttons, ribbons
- Brown, tan, black, white, and gray construction paper

Listening Center

- Theme-appropriate cassette tape and book: *Corduroy*

Writing Center

- Pencils with bear erasers
- Picture cards of characters in *Brown Bear, Brown Bear*
- Blank books with a bear on the cover
- Sentence strip headed with: My favorite type of bear is _____.

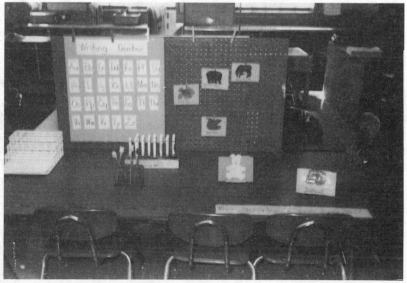

- Labeled picture cards of different kinds of bears: Koala, Grizzly, Panda, etc.

Block Center

- Variety of stuffed bears
- Plastic bear families (available in school supply catalogs)

Game Table

Button Collection Game

- Two game boards
- Two bear markers
- Die
- Button collection

Create two individual game boards by gluing a bear figure to the left side with paw prints that lead to a button. The child uses the die to determine how many times he may move his marker on the paw prints. The first child to reach the button may take a button from the button collection as a method of keeping score. This game can be correlated with the book *Corduroy*.

Sensory Table

- Water
- Two plastic ice cube trays
- Two plastic spoons
- Multicolored plastic Teddy bear counters

Encourage children to sort, classify, and count the bears.

GROUP TIME ACTIVITIES

These activities involve the whole class.

Oral Language Development

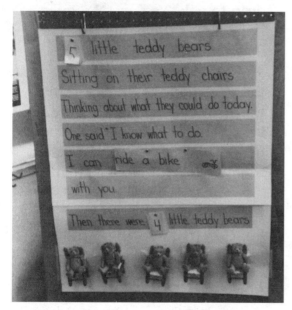

INTERACTIVE CHARTS

Five Little Teddy Bears
(To the tune: "Five Green and Speckled Frogs")

_____ little Teddy bears
Sitting on their Teddy chairs
Thinking about what they could do today.
One said "I know what to do.
I could _____ with you."
Then there were _____ little Teddy bears.

Create two sets of number cards for the first and last line of the song. (Note: The second number should be one less than the first number. See photo.) Provide blank sentence strips for the children to create verses for the other blank space in the song. Suggestions might include: "ride a bike," "play a game," etc.

Ten in the Bed

There were _____
in the bed
And the little one said,
"Roll over, Roll over."
So they all rolled over
and one fell out.

As a child turns the wheel, the numeral in the text matches the number of bear stickers in the window at the top of the chart. (See photo below.)

POEMS/SONGS/ FINGERPLAYS

Counting Song

One little, two little
Three little bears.
Four little, five little
Six little bears.
Seven little, eight little
Nine little bears.
Ten little _____ bears.

Children provide suggestions for the blank: Teddy, Koala, Panda, etc.

Bear Cheer

Bears are IN!
Bears are OUT!
Grab a bear and give a shout!
Give me a B.
Give me an E.
Give me an A.
Give me an R.
Give me an S.
What have you got?
BEARS!

FLANNEL BOARD STORY

Create felt pieces to retell *Brown Bear, Brown Bear, What Do You See?*

Literacy Development

✔ Ask children to brainstorm a list of what they know about bears.

✔ Create a Teddy bear attribute box by hiding a Teddy bear in a lidded box. Encourage the children to ask "Yes" or "No" questions about the contents. Write down all the questions you answered "Yes" to, and tape them to the outside of the box. This will help children deduce what's inside the box. Reveal the Teddy bear. This activity can serve as the introduction to the theme.

✔ Create verses for the interactive chart "Five Little Teddy Bears" on page 23.

✔ Sing the "Counting Song," on this page. Encourage children to contribute the names of different types of bears. Record these on sentence strips and display on subsequent singings of this song.

✔ Read *We're Going on a Bear Hunt*. With the children create motions to dramatize the action words.

✔ Dramatize *The Three Bears*.

✔ Read several versions of *The Three Bears*. Compare and contrast the versions. Record these comparisons on chart paper.

✔ Read *Where's My Teddy?* Before reading the last page, encourage the children to predict the ending. Record the predictions. Finish the reading. Ask the children: Which of your predictions came true?

✔ Ask children to dictate a group letter inviting their Teddy bears to a Teddy Bear Celebration. Record their dictation on chart paper. Encourage the children to listen for beginning or ending sounds of some of the words in their letter. Reproduce the letter and send home with each child.

✔ When the children bring their Teddy bears or stuffed animals to school, allow each child to introduce his or her bear to the class. Encourage others to ask questions about the bear: Where did it come from? How did you choose its name?

✔ Read *Brown Bear, Brown Bear*. Record the initial letter of a character on chart paper. Encourage the children to use letter knowledge to predict the character. Confirm by checking the text.

✔ Create a retelling of the class's favorite bear story. Ask the children to retell the story in their own words. Record their narrative.

EXTENSION ACTIVITIES

These extension activities can be used as individual assignments.

✔ Create *Corduroy* models: Allow the children to create a bear shape with geometric templates. Provide green paper to be cut into overalls and buttons to glue to the shoulder straps.

✔ Create a reproduction of *Brown Bear, Brown Bear*: Write the words of the text on large pieces of paper. Children can work individually or in cooperative groups to illustrate each page. Bind for a class book.

✔ Make an *Our Bear Day* Language-Experience Book. Each child draws a picture of their Teddy bear during Teddy Bear Day (see Literacy Development). Record each child's narrative and attach it to the child's picture. Bind for a class book.

✔ Invite the children to create self-portraits, and then use the language structure of *Brown Bear, Brown Bear* to create the text. Example: "Jessica, Jessica, Who do you see? I see Andy looking at me." The last page of the book can be small photographs of each child or a photo of the whole class with the words "I see the kindergarten looking at me."

MATH ACTIVITIES

✔ Provide a balance scale. Estimate if the children's bears weigh more, less, or the same as the teacher's bear. Confirm predictions by using balance scale. Sort and classify bears by weight.

✔ Ask children to make honey sandwiches with white and wheat bread. Create a group graph to depict how many students chose wheat bread, and how many chose white.

✔ Provide each child with a small bag of chocolate and vanilla bear-shaped cookies and a graph. Encourage the children to estimate the number of cookies in the bag and record their estimation on the back of the graph. Children may count the cookies and sort them into color piles. Then each child can color squares on the graph to correspond with the number of cookies.

✔ Help children measure their Teddy bears with unifix cubes. Compare the results. Arrange the unifix-cube "trains" from smallest to largest.

COOKING ACTIVITY

✔ Cook oatmeal, allowing each child to complete one part of the recipe.

SCIENCE ACTIVITY

✔ After discussing a variety of bear habitats, allow the children to choose a habitat to reproduce. Children work in cooperative groups with collage materials to recreate their chosen habitats.

BOOKLIST

Brown Bear, Brown Bear, What Do You See? by Bill Martin, Jr. (Henry Holt, 1983)

Corduroy by Don Freeman (Viking Press, 1968)

Emma's Pet by David McPhail (Dutton, 1985)

Ira Sleeps Over by Bernard Waber (Houghton Mifflin, 1973)

My Brown Bear Barney by Dorothy Butler (Greenwillow, 1989)

Teddy Bears' Picnic by Jimmy Kennedy (Peter Bedrick Books, 1987)

We're Going on a Bear Hunt by Michael Rosen (Macmillan, 1989)

Where's My Teddy? by Jez Alborough (Candlewick, 1992)

Who's in the Shed? by Brenda Parker (Rigby, 1987)

Clothes

Kindergartners always delight in the story *Caps For Sale*. Their continual interest was the force behind the Clothes unit. Since then, we have discovered a large variety of exciting and appropriate literature about clothing. I use this unit in place of a unit about colors, because so many of the clothing books incorporate color concepts.

AREA DESIGN

Sensory Table

- Water
- Soap bubbles
- Doll, baby clothes
- Washboard
- Drying rack, clothespins

Science Center

For Color Mixing
- Water
- Cups
- Food coloring
- Spoons for stirring

Game Table

The Clothes Line

Make two dresses out of white construction paper and glue them on to cardboard or oaktag. These will serve as your two game boards. Attach a piece of yarn above the dresses so it appears the dresses are hanging on a clothesline. Provide a basket of colored paper dresses, clothespins, and a die or spinner. The children can create their own rules to accompany the game materials. This game can be correlated with *Marianna May and Nursey*.

Listening Center

Theme-appropriate cassette tape and book: *Mary Wore a Red Dress*

GROUP TIME ACTIVITIES

These activities involve the whole class.

Oral Language Development

INTERACTIVE CHARTS

Clothes

_____wore a

_____

All day long.

Provide name cards for each child to place in the first blank. Provide cards of clothes choices for the second blank.

Monkeys, Monkeys

Monkeys, Monkeys
In the tree,
Throw the _____ cap
Down to me.

Create word cards of colors to complete the text.

SONGS/POEMS/ FINGERPLAYS

Seasonal Clothes

What do you wear on a _____(1)_____
day
When you can go out to play?
We wear _____(2)_____
On a _____(1)_____ day
When we can go out to play!

1: Type of day
2: Clothes worn on type of day mentioned in 1

Color Clothes

Will you wear red?
Oh my dear, oh my dear.
Will you wear red, today?
No I won't wear red
Because I'll have to go to bed.
No I won't wear red today!

FLANNEL BOARD STORY

Create felt pieces to correspond with *Marianna May and Nursey.*

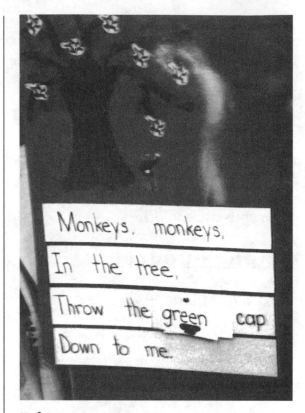

Literacy Development

✔ Read *Marianna May and Nursey.* Stop reading before the problem resolution. Ask the children to predict the resolution. Record all predictions. Finish the reading. Ask the children: Did the story's conclusion confirm your predictions?

✔ Make up new verses for the poem "Color Clothes." Encourage the children to contribute rhymes that make sense for each color word. Record all verses to use with subsequent uses.

✔ Read *Mary Wore a Red Dress.* Interact with the text by inserting a child's name and clothing into the pattern.

✔ Read *Ho Is for Hats.* With the children brainstorm a list of people who wear hats.

✔ Read and dramatize *Caps for Sale.*

These activities can be used as individual assignments.

✔ Paper Plate Hats: Create a hat from a paper plate. Decorate with collage materials (see Math).

✔ Class Clothesline: Children use watercolor paints or markers to draw their favorite item of clothing. Encourage the children to label the item on a card and attach it to the painting (Example: Krystal's Mickey Mouse dress, Steven's football pants). These can be displayed in the classroom by hanging a clothesline across a bulletin board and attaching the paintings with clothespins.

✔ Class version of *Mary Wore a Red Dress*: Each child draws a self-portrait using only a black crayon. They can then color in one item of clothing. Reproduce the sentence: _____ wore a _____ all day long. The children fill in the blanks to match their drawings. Bind the portraits into a class book.

✔ Tye-Dye T-shirts: After reading *Marianna May and Nursey*, ask each child to contribute a white T-shirt from their home. Demonstrate tye-dyeing procedures and have each child tye-dye their T-shirt.

MATH ACTIVITIES

✔ Create a T-shirt color graph. After the children have dyed their T-shirts, create a graph demonstrating which colors they chose for this project.

✔ Create a hat decoration store. Provide various collage materials appropriate for hat creations. Label each item with a price ranging from 1 to 3 cents each. For example: Cotton ball is 1 cent each, ribbons are 2 cents each, etc. Provide each child with 10 pennies to spend at the hat store. The children use these items to create hats (see Extension Activity on page 31).

BOOKLIST

Caps for Sale by Esphyr Slobodkina (Scholastic, 1981)

Crazy Clothes by Niki Yektai (Bradbury, 1988)

Ho Is for Hats by William Jay Smith (Little, Brown, 1989)

Marianna May and Nursey by Tomie de Paola (Holiday House, 1983)

Mary Wore Her Red Dress and Henry Wore His Green Sneakers by Merle Peek (Clarion, 1985)

Mrs. Honey's Hat by Pam Adams (Child's Play Ltd. 1980)

A New Dress for Maya by Malorie Blackman (Garth Stevens Children's Books, 1991)

Eggs

One year, a child in my class had relatives who owned a farm. The relatives volunteered an incubator and fertilized eggs, and provided a home for the newly-hatched chicks. And so began this Egg unit. Since that time, our class has discovered wonderful literature about all the other animals that hatch from eggs besides chickens. These days, we continue to learn from the Egg unit—with or without an incubator!

AREA DESIGN

Art Center

- Feathers
- Eggshells
- Bird templates

Listening Center

- Theme-appropriate cassette tape and book: *Green Eggs and Ham*

Writing Center

- Picture cards of animals in *Seven Eggs*
- Small blank books with eggs on the cover and the sentence from *Seven Eggs*: The egg cracked and out came a _____.
- Pencils with a small plastic egg glued to the top

Science Center

- Nests
- Magnifying glass
- Books about nests and birds

Easel

- Paper cut in an oval shape

Game Table

- Two purchased nests
- Plastic eggs
- Two tongs
- Spinner or die

Children invent their own games using these items.

Sensory Table

- 12 plastic eggs
- Plastic loam egg carton
- Tongs

GROUP TIME ACTIVITIES

These activities involve the whole class.

Oral Language Development

INTERACTIVE CHART

I Found a Little Egg One Day

I found a little egg one day
And out hatched a ____(1)____.
What do you think I heard it say?
____(2)____.

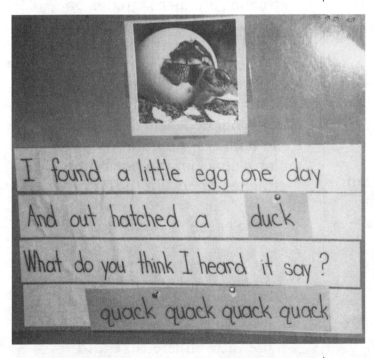

Create word cards for the blank spaces.

1: Animal name
2: Sound that animal makes.

POEMS/SONGS/FINGERPLAYS

Five Baby Chicks

Five white eggs.
One, two, three, four, five.
Five little taps.
One, two, three, four, five.
How many chicks come out alive?
One, two, three, four, five.

Ten Fluffy Chicks

Five eggs and five eggs
That makes ten.
Sitting on top is Mother Hen.
Crackle, crackle, crackle.
What do I see?
Ten fluffy chicks
Looking at me!

Baby Birdy

Here's a baby birdy
Hatching from his shell.
Out comes his head,
Then comes his tail.
Then his legs he stretches,
His wings he gives a flap.
Then he flies and flies.
Now what do you think
of that?

FLANNEL BOARD STORY

Create felt pieces to retell *Seven Eggs*.

Literacy Development

✔ With the children, list animals that hatch from eggs.

✔ Innovate new verses for the interactive chart "I Found a Little Egg One Day."

✔ Dramatize animals that hatch from eggs.

✔ Read *Seven Eggs*. Stop reading before the last page of the story. Encourage the children to predict the ending. Finish reading the story so children can alter or confirm their predictions.

✔ Read *Chickens Aren't the Only Ones*. Ask the children: Which animals hatch from eggs? Add children's ideas to the list.

✔ Read *The Little Red Hen* and *The Little Yellow Chicken*. Encourage the class to compare and contrast the two books. Record these comparisons on chart paper.

EXTENSION ACTIVITIES

These extension activities can be used as individual assignments.

✔ Create a personal chart of "I Found a Little Egg One Day" (see Oral Language Development). Each child cuts out an egg shape from white paper, then cuts it in half and attaches a paper fastener on one side so that the egg opens. The child then draws an animal that hatches from an egg and glues the picture onto the egg so that it is exposed when the egg is opened. The child writes the name of the animal in the blank space of the poem and attaches the poem to the egg.

✔ Create eggshell collages.

✔ Have the children help make a big book version of *Seven Eggs*. Children can work with partners to illustrate one page, attach the text and bind for a class book.

✔ Invite children to paint their favorite egg-hatching animals. Cut out a large egg from bulletin board paper, staple the egg and the children's paintings to the bulletin board.

✔ Color hard-boiled eggs. Brush liquid starch on the egg. Apply small squares of tissue paper. Peel off the tissue. This creates a marble effect on the egg shell.

✔ Have students draw Humpty Dumpty on their hard-boiled eggs.

COOKING ACTIVITIES

✔ After reading *Green Eggs and Ham*, make green scrambled eggs using green food coloring.

✔ After completing the hard-boiled egg projects from Extension Activities, the children can prepare egg salad.

MATH ACTIVITIES

✔ Send home a note asking each child to bring a hard-boiled egg to school. Suggest that the parents and children discuss ways that the eggs could be brought to school without getting cracked. Graph the different ways the children brought their eggs to school.

✔ Estimate the number of malted-milk ball eggs in a jar and count them.

BOOKLIST

Chickens Aren't the Only Ones by Ruth Heller (Putnam, 1981)

Egg to Chick by Millicent Selsam (Harper Collins, 1987)

Fancy That! by Pamela Allen (Orchard Books, 1988)

Good Morning Chick by Mirra Ginsburg (William Morrow, 1989)

Green Eggs and Ham by Dr. Seuss (Random House, 1960)

Hatch by Karyn Henly (Carolrhoda Books, 1980)

The Little Yellow Chicken by Joy Cowley (The Wright Group, 1988)

Seven Eggs by Meredith Hooper (Harper Collins, 1983)

Fall

The magic of leaves changing colors fascinates children. Watching their enjoyment of the season, it seemed only natural to develop a unit about fall. Exploring autumn is also an effective way to integrate science and color words into a kindergarten program in a meaningful context.

AREA DESIGN

Dramatic Play

Pumpkin Farm
(This activity is most effective following a field trip.)

GENERAL PROPS
- Pumpkins of various sizes
- Cash register
- Indian corn, gourds, nuts, and other autumn favorites
- Empty plastic cider containers
- Small wagon with hay to replicate a hayride
- Plastic garden tools, buckets, hose

PROPS TO ENCOURAGE LITERACY
- Stickers for price tags
- Order pads
- Sign stating the price of the pumpkins
- Sign denoting the time of the hayrides
- Sign-up sheet for the hayrides
- Guest register
- Books about pumpkins or farms

Writing Center

- Blank books with an apple on their covers
- Labeled picture cards of different types of leaves
- Sentence strip headed with: My favorite type of leaf is _____.

- Fall Word Bank: Child-generated words that describe fall. (Example: leaves, rake, jump, cold, sweaters, etc.)

Art Center

- Leaves
- Leaf templates
- Variety of papers in fall colors: yellow, orange, brown, etc.
- Dried pumpkin seeds
- Acorns

Science Center

- Variety of autumn favorites: small pumpkins, gourds, acorns, colorful leaves, etc.
- Magnifying glass
- Paper and pencils to record observations
- Books about fall

Game Table

Red Leaf, Yellow Leaf

- Game board created from a large piece of poster board with a tree drawn on it
- Yellow and red leaf cut-outs
- Spinner or die

Children create their own rules for the game using these materials. This can be correlated with the book *Red Leaf, Yellow Leaf.*

Sensory Table

- Water
- Plastic apples/pumpkins
- Empty plastic half-gallon apple cider containers
- Plastic spoons
- Plastic colanders

Listening Center

- Theme-appropriate cassette tape and book: *The Seasons of Arnold's Apple Tree*

GROUP TIME ACTIVITIES

These activities involve the whole class.

Oral Language Activities

INTERACTIVE CHARTS

Leaves Falling Down

_____ leaves falling down.
_____ leaves falling down.
Over all the town.
Over all the town.

Provide pairs of color words for the blank spaces in the poem. Choose color words that match fall leaf colors.

The Orchard

The orchard has so many trees
More than I've ever seen.
They are full of apples
Red, yellow, and green.

Create word cards for the children to match to the color words in the chart.

Hibernation

Where do the _____ go when leaves turn red?
They crawl in the _____ and go to bed.
They hibernate, they hibernate,
And they don't come out until spring.

Create pairs of word cards for blank spaces in the chart. For example, turtles/pond, bears/cave, foxes/den.

POEMS/SONGS/FINGERPLAYS

Farmer Brown
(Traditional song)

Farmer Brown had five red apples
hanging in his tree.
Farmer Brown had five red apples
hanging in his tree.
He picked one apple
And ate it hungrily.
Then Farmer Brown had four red
apples hanging in his tree.

Jack-o-Faces

This is Jack-o-Happy.
This is Jack-o-Sad.
Now you see him sleepy.
Now you see him mad.
This is Jack in pieces small.
But in a pie he is best of all!

Way Up High

Way up high in the apple tree,
Two little apples were smiling at me.
I shook that tree as hard as I could.
Down came the apples.
MMMMMM, were they good.

Leaves Falling Down

All the leaves are falling down
Yellow, orange, and red.
They pitter patter to the ground
One fell on my head!

A-P-P-L-E-S
(To the tune: "Bingo")

There was a farmer who had
a tree,
And guess what grew upon it?
A-P-P-L-E-S
A-P-P-L-E-S
A-P-P-L-E-S
Some apples grew upon it.

Gray Squirrel

Gray squirrel, gray squirrel,
Swish your bushy tail.
Gray squirrel, gray squirrel,
Swish your bushy tail.
Wrinkle up your funny nose.
Put a nut between your toes.
Gray squirrel, gray squirrel
Swish your bushy tail.

FLANNEL BOARD STORY

Create felt pieces and felt numbers to retell the song "Farmer Brown" on page 41.

Literacy Development

✔ With the children, brainstorm a list of what they know about fall.

✔ Create an autumn attribute box by hiding mittens, a scarf, and a warm hat in a lidded box. Have children ask "Yes" or "No" questions about the contents. Record correct guesses on the side of the box. Children guess the contents based on the recorded responses. Reveal the contents. Children can generate a list of other items that are needed in the fall.

✔ With the children, generate motions to accompany "Jack-o-Faces" on page 41.

✔ Read *Sleepy Bear* and discuss hibernation. With the children, create word cards for the "Hibernation" chart on page 41.

✔ Read *When Autumn Comes*. With the children, list the autumn changes covered in the book. Take a Fall Walk with the children. Add their observations to the list.

EXTENSION ACTIVITIES

These extension activities can be used as individual assignments.

✔ Cut four tree shapes from brown paper. Label each tree with the name of a season. Allow the children to use collage materials to depict the four seasons.

✔ After the children have created a tree using brown and green construction paper, print apples on the branches with half of an apple that has been dipped into paint. Duplicate the sentence from the "Farmer Brown" poem as follows: Farmer _____ has _____ red apples hanging in a tree. Each child completes the sentence by writing his or her name in the first blank and the number of apple prints in the second blank. Attach this sentence to the apple tree.

✔ After the children have taken a walk focusing on fall changes (see Literacy Development), create a mural by cutting trees from brown construction paper and attaching these to a large piece of bulletin board paper. The children add the fall leaves by tearing appropriate colors of tissue paper. Each child can then add a self-portrait to the mural. Transcribe's each child's observations about fall onto paper, cut into a speech-balloon shape, and attached to the self-portrait.

✔ Ask children to slowly drop red, green, yellow, and orange food coloring into a coffee filter. Colors will blend together at edges and create new colors. The children can trace and cut a leaf shape on to the dried filter to create a fall leaf.

✔ Cook apple sauce, or any apple or pumpkin recipe.

✔ Visit a pumpkin farm or apple orchard and write a thank-you letter.

✔ Pumpkin Farm Language-Experience Book: After a class field trip, have each child illustrate one aspect of the trip. Record the child's dictation at the bottom of the paper. The children sequence the pages to replicate the sequence of events during the trip. Bind for a class book.

✔ Reproduce the poem "Jack-o-Faces." Children can add illustrations and sequence the pages to create an individual book.

✔ Reproduce the interactive chart "Leaves Falling Down" on page 41. Provide squares of colored paper for children to record the color words for the blank spaces. Personal illustrations can be added to the chart to depict fall leaves.

MATH ACTIVITIES

✔ Ask each child to provide a collection of fall leaves. Use these to create a graph.

✔ After tasting red, yellow, and green apples, graph the children's favorite type of apple.

✔ Ask each child to bring an apple to school. Sort and classify the apples according to color, size, weight, number of bruises, etc. Ask the children to suggest other categories for sorting and classifying.

✔ Use apples to measure things in the room, e.g., The table is _____ apples long. My friend is _____ apples tall.

BOOKLIST

Apples and Pumpkins by Anne Rockwell (Scholastic, 1989)

Autumn Days by Ann Schweninger (Penguin, 1991)

Good Night Owl by Pat Hutchins (Collier Books, 1972)

My Apple Tree by Harriet Ziefert (HarperCollins, 1991)

Nuts to You by Lois Ehlert (Harcout Brace Jovanovich, 1993)

The Pumpkin Patch by Elizabeth King (Dutton, 1990)

Pumpkins by Mary Lyn Ray (Harcourt Brace Jovanovich, 1993)

Red Leaf, Yellow Leaf by Lois Ehlert (Scholastic, 1991)

The Seasons of Arnold's Apple Tree by Gail Gibbons (Harcourt Brace Jovanovich, 1984)

Ska-Tat by Kimberly Knutson (MacMillan, 1993)

Sleepy Bear by Lydia Dobcovich (Trumpet Club, 1982)

When Autumn Comes by Robert Maas (Henry Holt, 1991)

Food

Every year our class eagerly anticipates this unit—we transform our dramatic play area into a child-size version of a pizzeria, discover many wonderful books about pizza and other foods, visit a local pizza restaurant, and make pizza in the classroom! It is no wonder why the Food unit gains popularity each year.

AREA DESIGN

Dramatic Play

Restaurant

GENERAL PROPS
- Child-sized stove, refrigerator
- Plastic food
- Cooking utensils, tables and chairs, aprons, cash register

PROPS TO ENCOURAGE LITERACY
- Menus, order pads, telephone and telephone book
- Coupons, posters and place mats from local restaurants; cookbooks; recipe cards; reservation book; pocket chart reading: Today's special is _____.
- Pictures of food
- Signs on hanging clips labeled: Place order here.

Art Center

- Food pictures from magazines for collages
- Styrofoam meat trays
- Tin pie pans
- Fruit and vegetable templates for tracing
- Dried beans for gluing

Listening Center

- Theme-appropriate cassette tape and book: *If You Give a Mouse a Cookie*

Writing Center

- Labeled food cards
- Sentence taped to center: My favorite food is_____.
- Pencils with theme-related toppers
- Blank books with theme-related stickers on the covers

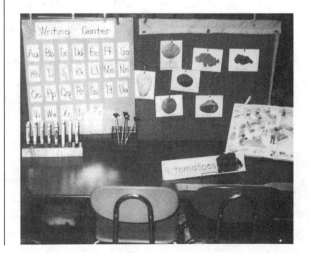

Block Center

- Plastic mixing bowls and measuring cups for building

Easel

- Various vegetables for creating vegetable prints

Science Center

- Place a stalk of celery in colored water.
- Provide paper and pencils for children to record their predictions.
- Place small pieces of food into empty film canisters. Punch holes in the lids. Choose items with distinctive scents: peanuts, lemons, cinnamon. Children smell the contents and match a word or picture card to the canister.

Game Table

Pepperoni Pizza

Create two large "pizza" circles from brown cardboard. On each "pizza" trace 12 smaller circles. Provide a basket of red "pepperoni" circles (to be placed on "pizzas") and a die. Children toss the die and place a corresponding number of "pepperoni" onto their pizza. The child who covers his or her "pizza" first, wins. Tie in this game with *Little Nino's Pizzeria*.

Sensory Table

- Plastic fruits and vegetables
- Small brushes for scrubbing
- Liquid soap and water
- Plastic tongs and spoons

GROUP TIME ACTIVITIES

These activities involve the whole class.

Oral Language Development

INTERACTIVE CHARTS

Pickles

My mother gave me a nickel
To buy a pickle,
But I didn't buy a pickle
I bought some _____.

Create food word cards for the blank.

Pickles

My mother gave me a nickel

To buy a pickle.

But I didn't buy a pickle.

I bought some grapes.

The Food Song

_____, _____
Yum! Yum! Yum!
Don't you wish that you had some?

_____, _____
Tastes so fine.
I could eat it all the time!

Fill in the blanks with names of foods.

Food

_____ is yummy.
_____ is hot.
_____ tastes best when you eat a lot!

Create sets of three matching word cards to fill in the blank spaces in the text.

SONGS/POEMS/FINGERPLAYS

Who Stole the Cookie?
(Traditional chant)

Who stole the cookie from the cookie jar?
_____ stole the cookie from the cookie jar.
Who me?
Yes, you!
Couldn't be.
Then, who?

Use students' names for blank spaces.

Pizza Song
(To the tune: Oscar Myer Wiener Theme Song)

Oh, I wish I was a _____ pizza.
That is what I'd really love to be.
Cause if I was a _____ pizza,
Everyone would take a bite of me!

Children fill in the blanks with favorite pizza toppings.

Picnic Song

Going on a picnic,
Leaving right away
If it doesn't rain,
We'll stay all day.
Do you have the _____?
Yes, I have the _____.
Here we go!

Children suggest picnic foods for blank spaces.

See, See, See

See, see, see,
What colors do I see?
Purple plums, bright red tomatoes,
Yellow corn, big brown potatoes,
Bright green lettuce,
yum, yum, good.
I see colors in my food.

Chocolate

Chocolate ice cream,
Chocolate cake,
Chocolate cookies,
Chocolate shake,
Chocolate bagels,
Chocolate steak,
Make a chocolate belly ache!

Pancakes

Mix a pancake,
Stir a pancake,
Pop it in a pan.
Fry the pancake,
Toss the pancake,
Catch it if you can!

FLANNEL BOARD STORY

Cut out flannel shapes to retell the story *Stone Soup*. This can also be retold with plastic items and a large soup pot.

Literacy Development

✔ Read *Little Nino's Pizzeria*. With the children, brainstorm a list of possible toppings for pizza. Use this list to complete the text of "Pizza Song" on page 48.

✔ Read *Peanut Butter and Jelly*. With the children, create an innovation titled, "Pepperoni Pizza." Allow the children to generate suggestions for creating a pizza. Record all suggestions.

✔ Read *Stone Soup*. Dramatize the story using appropriate props.

✔ Brainstorm and record a recipe for cooking stone soup.

✔ Read different versions of *Stone Soup*. Encourage the class to compare and contrast books. Record these comparisons on chart paper.

✔ Read *Pancakes for Breakfast*. Encourage the children to compose the text for this wordless picture book.

✔ With the children, create new items for the blank space in "Pickles" on page 47.

✔ Read *The Great Big Enormous Turnip*. With the children, list the characters from the story. Cut the list apart to create individual character cards. Distribute these to the class members and dramatize the story.

✔ Read *I Like*. Using the text as a model, record foods that the children like by completing the sentence: I like _____.

EXTENSION ACTIVITIES

These extension activities can be used as an individual assignment.

✔ After reading a variety of pizza books and learning a variety of pizza songs (see Oral Language Development and Literacy Development) create paper pizzas. The children trace and cut a brown paper circle and glue it to the center of a paper plate. Provide additional colored paper to be cut into topping shapes and small pieces of yellow yarn for cheese.

✔ Provide a variety of fruits and vegetables which have been cut in half. These can be dipped into paint and used to create food prints.

✔ Create individual *I Like* books. Duplicate the repetitive sentence, "I like _____," and have the children create their own words for the blank space. Words can be illustrated with markers, crayons, or pictures from magazines.

✔ Give each child a photocopy of the pickle song on page 47. Have the children create their own word cards for the blank space.

✔ After reading a variety of pancake books and learning the pancake poem on page 49, create Styrofoam™ pancakes. The children trace two circles onto a white Styrofoam™ meat tray. Color these brown and cut them out. Glue the "pancakes" to a paper plate. Create butter squares following the same procedure. Mix brown tempera paint with white glue and pour over the pancakes. This dries clear and gives the appearance of syrup. Reproduce and attach the pancake poem to the pancake displays.

MATH ACTIVITIES

✔ Read *The Doorbell Rang*. Recreate the story with real cookies. Record these equations onto chart paper.

✔ Graph the children's favorite foods. Prepare and sample the most popular choice.

✔ Ask each child to contribute one fresh vegetable for the making of *Stone Soup*. Sort and classify the vegetables according to color, size, shape, etc.

COOKING ACTIVITY

✔ Provide the ingredients for making pizza and make a pizza! Take photographs of the children during this process. Use these snapshots to create a class book, or for the class game of "Pepperoni Pizza" on page 47.

FIELD TRIPS

✔ Visit a local restaurant or bakery.

✔ Visit a local grocery store. Each child can contribute a small amount of money to buy the ingredients for a class cooking project, such as a salad, fruit shakes, soup.

BOOKLIST

Chicken Soup with Rice by Maurice Sendak (Scholastic, 1962)

Eating the Alphabet by Lois Ehlert (Trumpet Club, 1989)

The Great Big Enormous Turnip by Alexei Tolstoy (Scott Foresman, 1976)

Green Bananas by Pam Neville and Andrea Butler (Rigby, 1988)

Gregory, the Terrible Eater by Mitchell Sharmat (Scholastic, 1980)

I Like by Jillian Cutting (The Wright Group, 1988)

If You Give a Mouse a Cookie by Laura Joffe Numeroff (Scholastic, 1985)

Little Nino's Pizzeria by Karen Barbour (Harcourt Brace Javanovich, 1987)

Lunch by Denise Fleming (Henry Holt, 1992)

The Magic Porridge Pot by Paul Galdone (Clarion, 1979)

Pancakes for Breakfast by Tomie dePaola (Harcourt Brace Jovanovich, 1978)

Peanut Butter and Jelly by Nadine Bernard Westcott (Trumpet Club 1987)

Stone Soup by Ann McGovern (Scholastic, 1968)

Today Is Monday by Eric Carle (Scholastic, 1993)

The Gingerbread Man

The traditional tale of *The Gingerbread Man* is great for sharing during the holidays—a time filled with family traditions. During this time, I encourage the children to bring their families' favorite books to share with their friends. In addition to introducing the children to traditional tales, this unit provides opportunities for comparing and contrasting the many Gingerbread Man versions, and exploring other themes such as home, family, and friends.

AREA DESIGN

Dramatic Play

Bakery

GENERAL PROPS
- Child-sized stove and refrigerator
- Mixing bowls
- Cookie sheets, baking supplies, pot holders
- Plastic doughnuts, cakes, cookies

PROPS TO ENCOURAGE LITERACY
- Cookbooks, recipe cards and file box
- Order pads, pencils
- Boxes or bags from local bakery
- Chart reading: Today's Specials Are _____.

- Labeled pictures of bakery foods
- Empty cake mix, cookie, and brownie boxes

Writing Center

- Labeled picture cards of characters from *The Gingerbread Man*
- Sentence strip reading: Have you written to the Gingerbread Man?
- Mailbox for letters to the Gingerbread Man
- Envelopes, stationery
- Sentence strip reading: Dear Gingerbread Man

Block Center

- Plastic Bowls
- Wooden spoons

Art Center

- Gingerbread men templates
- Plastic cookie cutters for tracing
- Colored glue
- Ribbons, sequins, glitter

Listening Center

Cassette tape and book of *The Gingerbread Man*

Science Center

- Basket of a variety of nuts in shells
- Labeled word cards of nut type: almond, pecan, walnut, etc.
- Sorting tray
- Tongs for sorting
- Variety of spices placed in film canisters with small holes punched at the top
- Fresh ginger root or dried ginger

Game Table

Create a path game based on *The Gingerbread Man.* Create directions

for the board game asking children to "collect" or "remove" Gingerbread Man characters. The characters from the story can be attached to the game with Velcro™. Players remove or collect characters according to directions on the board.

Sensory Table

- Water
- Variety of mixing bowls, plastic spoons, etc.
- Sponges, scrub brushes, towels
- Empty liquid soap bottles

GROUP TIME ACTIVITIES

These activities involve the whole class.

Oral Language Development

INTERACTIVE CHART

The Gingerbread Man
(To the tune: "London Bridge")

When she mixes gingerbread,
It turns into a man instead
With frosting collar around his throat
And raisin buttons on his coat.

Create word cards that children match to words in the rhyme. Attach a flannel gingerbread man to the chart. Provide flannel buttons, eyes, mouth, and nose in order for the children to create a gingerbread man as they use the chart. A wooden spoon can be provided to be used as a pointer.

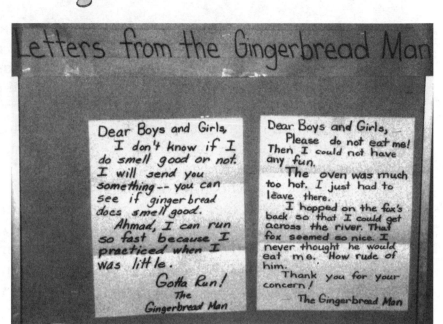

Letters from the Gingerbread Man

Dear Boys and Girls,
I don't know if I do smell good or not. I will send you something-- you can see if gingerbread does smell good.
Ahmad, I can run so fast because I practiced when I was little.
Gotta Run!
The Gingerbread Man

Dear Boys and Girls,
Please do not eat me! Then I could not have any fun.
The oven was much too hot. I just had to leave there.
I hopped on the fox's back so that I could get across the river. That fox seemed so nice. I never thought he would eat me. How rude of him.
Thank you for your concern!
The Gingerbread Man

SONG

The Gingerbread Man
(To the tune: "Pop Goes The Weasel")

Who can catch the Gingerbread Man?
Catch him if you can.
I can catch him said the_____.
But away he ran.

For the blank, add names of characters in the tale, or people in the neighborhood: butcher, florist, etc.

FLANNEL BOARD STORY

Create felt pieces to retell *The Gingerbread Man*.

Literacy Development

✔ Write a letter with the children to the Gingerbread Man. Encourage the children to ask questions. This activity can be done throughout the unit, with the Gingerbread Man writing back to the children and asking questions about the classroom. Encourage the children to write individual letters using materials at the Writing Center (see Area Design).

✔ Compare and contrast different versions of *The Gingerbread Man*. Graph your answers.

✔ Create word cards for the song, *The Gingerbread Man* and act it out.

✔ Place all the ingredients for gingerbread in a large basket. Discuss the ingredients. Ask the children what they could make with these ingredients. Record all responses. Show the children a recipe for gingerbread. Prepare the gingerbread, with each child completing one task in the recipe.

EXTENSION ACTIVITIES

These extension activities can be used as individual assignments.

✔ Each child traces and cuts out a gingerbread man shape. Decorate with Goop.

✔ Mix 1 cup water, 1 cup salt, and 1 cup flour. Place in several squeeze bottles. Add a few drops of food coloring into each bottle and mix. The children squeeze the goop on to the gingerbread men. When it dries the goop replicates frosting.

✔ With the children brainstorm the characters and setting from the story. Each child illustrates one component of the story. Help the children to sequence their illustrations while you attach them to bulletin board paper to replicate the story.

✔ Mix 4 cups flour, 1 cup salt, and 1 1/2 cups warm water. Children roll dough and cut out gingerbread men with cookie cutters.

✔ Mix together: 1 pound powdered sugar, 1/2 tsp. cream of tartar, and 3 egg whites. Beat with hand mixer until stiff. Each child uses mixture to frost a small milk carton. Decorate with small candies. Mixture gets very hard as it dries. Attach the sentence "We read the Gingerbread Man" to each house.

MATH ACTIVITY

✔ After each child has eaten a gingerbread man cookie, graph which part they ate first: The head, a leg, or an arm.

BOOKLIST

The Gingerbread Boy by Paul Galdone (Clarion, 1975)

The Gingerbread Boy by Sue Kassirer (Random House, 1993)

The Gingerbread Man by Eric A. Kimmel (Holiday House, 1993)

The Gingerbread Man by Karen Schmidt (Scholastic, 1967)

Halloween

Over the years, the children's favorite books during Halloween are the books about friendly monsters. Their enthusiasm for the holiday inspired me to develop it into a thematic unit. The literature supports drama and active imaginations, and the literature extensions are a wonderful way to introduce kindergartners to a variety of art mediums.

AREA DESIGN

Dramatic Play

Puppet Theater

GENERAL PROPS
- Puppet theater
- Puppets
- Cash register

PROPS TO ENCOURAGE LITERACY
- Tickets
- Sentence strip: Admission: 50¢
- Sentence strip: Today's show is
  _____.
- Materials to create a program: paper, crayons, markers, pencils
- Familiar story books to dramatize

Art Center

- Circle templates, orange paper, and green yarn to create pumpkins
- Dried pumpkin seeds
- Black and orange yarn scraps
- Paper bags and collage materials to create puppets

Easel

- Black, orange, yellow, and brown paint

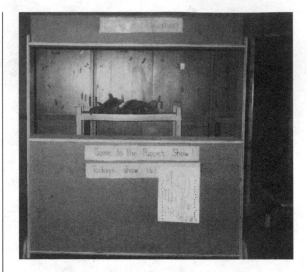

Listening Center

- Theme-appropriate cassette tape and book: *Where The Wild Things Are*

Writing Center

- Word cards for Halloween creatures and features: skeleton, witch, monster, etc.
- Blank books made from black and orange construction paper
- Pencils with pumpkins glued to the tops

- Halloween rubber stamps with matching labeled word cards

Science Center

- Variety of pumpkins
- Books about pumpkins
- Basket of unifix cubes
- Paper with sentence: My pumpkin is _____ unifix cubes tall.
- Magnifying glasses
- Pumpkin seeds

Game Table

- Small plastic pumpkins
- Two games boards depicting pumpkin vines
- Spinner or die

Children create their own rules for the game using the above materials.

Sensory Table

- Rice
- Two plastic hollow pumpkins
- A variety of plastic funnels
- Plastic scoops

GROUP TIME ACTIVITIES

These activities involve the whole class.

Oral Language Development

INTERACTIVE CHARTS

Halloween

I know there are no _____
That go flying through the air,
But I pretend on Halloween
That they are really there.

Create word cards of Halloween characters for the blank space in the chart: ghosts, witches, monsters, etc.

Ten Little Wild Things

___ little wild things
Swinging on a vine
One fell off and began to whine
_____ called the doctor
And the doctor said
"Put those wild things into bed!"

Create number cards for the first blank and word cards of the children's name for the second blank. This can be correlated with *Where The Wild Things Are.*

POEMS/SONGS/ FINGERPLAYS

One Little Monster
(To the tune: "Ten Little Indians")

One little, two little, three little monsters
Four little, five little, six little monsters
Seven little, eight little, nine little monsters
Ten of them can't scare me!

If You Ever See A Monster
(To the tune: "If You Ever See a Lassie")

If you ever see a monster,
A big, ugly monster.
If you ever see a monster,
Here's what you do.
Make this face,
And this face.
Make this face,
And this face.
If you ever see a monster,
Be sure to shout "BOO!"

Children can make silly faces as they sing song.

Pumpkin Man
(To the tune: "Do You Know the Muffin Man?")

Do you know the Pumpkin Man?
The Pumpkin Man, the Pumpkin Man?
Do you know the Pumpkin Man
Who lives in a pumpkin patch?

Meanies
(To the tune: a variation of "Twinkle Twinkle Little Star")

Where do Meanies live?
Where do Meanies live?
Meanies live in garbage cans.
Meanies live in garbage cans.
That's where Meanies live.

FLANNEL BOARD STORY

Create felt pieces to retell a Halloween story.

Literacy Development

✔ Read *Maggie and the Monster* and *There's an Alligator under My Bed*. Discuss the warning signs written by the characters in the book. Encourage the children to brainstorm warning statements. Record these statements.

✔ Dramatize *Where the Wild Things Are*.

✔ Compare and contrast a Meanie and A Wild Thing. Record the children's observations on chart paper.

✔ With the children, innovate new verses for the song *The Pumpkin Man* (on page 60). Record the new verses on sentence strips for subsequent singings. Examples might include: Have you seen a scary witch who lives in a haunted house?

✔ Read *The Monsters' Party* by Joy Cowley. With the children, list the activities from the story. Dramatize the story. Encourage the children to generate new actions for the monsters to perform. Dramatize again, including the new actions.

✔ Cover a small box with dark paper and fill it with Halloween treats. Then read *In a Dark Dark Wood*. Stop reading before the final page. Show children the small box and ask them to predict the contents. Record students' guesses on the side of the box. Finish reading the book, and then open the box. Were their predictions right? Children can take home the treats.

- ✔ Read *Meanies* by Joy Cowley. With the children, list attributes of a Meanie.

- ✔ Compare and contrast *In A Dark Dark Wood* and *A Dark Dark Tale*. Record children's ideas on chart paper.

- ✔ Ask students to describe how to carve a pumpkin. Use this sequence list to create task cards. Allow the children to each choose a card. In sequence, each child follows the written directions on the card to perform the task.

- ✔ With the children, innovate new Halloween words for the interactive chart "Halloween" on page 59. Record the new words and use them on subsequent singings.

EXTENSION ACTIVITIES

These activities can be used as individual assignments.

- ✔ Children use collage materials to create a creature. Construction paper bodies can be attached to paper plate heads.

- ✔ Each child generates a warning sign (see Literacy Development).

Signs can be attached to individual "wild things."

- ✔ After carving a pumpkin, use the left-over pumpkin pieces to create stamps. Dip the pieces in orange paint and print on dark paper. Designs can be carved into the pieces by an adult using scissors or a knife.

MATH ACTIVITIES

- ✔ Encourage each child to estimate the circumference of the class pumpkin by cutting a piece of string long enough to fit around the pumpkin. Sort the strings into three groups: Too long, too short, and just right.

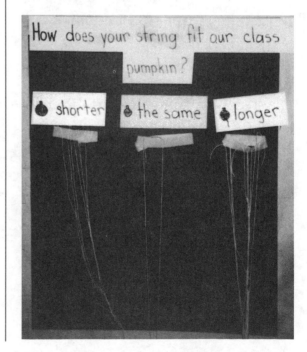

✔ Encourage children to guess the weight of the class pumpkin. Record guesses. Leave a bathroom scale out for the children to weigh the pumpkin.

✔ Estimate the number of seeds in the class pumpkin.

✔ Dramatize the interactive chart "Ten Little Wild Things" on page 60.

✔ Create Halloween patterns using unifix cubes.

✔ Create a class graph to indicate the class preference for the pumpkin carving. Should the pumpkin have a scary face or a happy face?

✔ Create a class graph to demonstrate the class's favorite Halloween stories.

COOKING ACTIVITY

✔ Make pumpkin bread (or anything pumpkin!).

BOOKLIST

Andrew's Amazing Monsters by Kathryn Hook Berlan (Atheneum, 1993)

A Dark Dark Tale by Ruth Brown (Dial, 1981)

Go Away Big Green Monster by Ed Emberley (Little, Brown, 1992)

In a Dark Dark Wood by June Melser and Joy Cowley (The Wright Group, 1980)

Maggie and the Monster by Elizabeth Winthrop (Holiday House, 1987)

Meanies by Joy Cowley (The Wright Group, 1983)

The Monsters' Party by Joy Cowley (The Wright Group, 1981)

One Hungry Monster by Susan Heyboer O'Keefe (Scholastic, 1992)

There's a Nightmare in My Closet by Mercer Mayer (Dial, 1985)

There's an Alligator under My Bed by Mercer Mayer (Dial, 1987)

Where the Wild Things Are by Maurice Sendak (Harper Trophy, 1963)

The Old Lady Who Swallowed a Fly

This unit was created by the children! They began to make connections about books with an "old lady" theme. I'm certain that this unit's popularity is based on the fact that the books and activities were chosen and created by kindergartners.

AREA DESIGN

Game Table

Old Lady Board Game

Create two game boards that picture all the characters from the story *The Old Lady Who Swallowed a Fly*. Create a double set of cards which illustrate each character. The players use a spinner or die to determine the number of cards they will pick up. As they collect a card, they match it to the character on their individual game board. The player to match all the characters first, is the winner.

Sensory Table

- Plastic flies
- Small nets

Listening Center

- Theme-appropriate cassette tape and book: *Strega Nona*

GROUP TIME ACTIVITIES

These activities involve the whole class.

Oral Language Development

INTERACTIVE CHART

The Old Lady

There was an old lady who swallowed a _____.

Create picture and word cards for the blank space. (See photo at right).

SONGS/POEMS/ FINGERPLAYS

Mother Goose Rhymes

✔ Recite "There Was an Old Woman Who Lived in a Shoe."

✔ Recite "Old Mother Hubbard."

FLANNEL BOARD STORY

Create felt pieces to correspond with *The Little Old Lady Who Wasn't Afraid of Anything.*

Literacy Development

✔ Read *The Old Lady Who Swallowed a Fly.* Allow the children to brainstorm motions for each line of the poem so they can act it out.

✔ Read *Mrs. Wishy Washy* by Joy Cowley. With the children, list the characters from the story. Cut apart this list to create individual name tags. Allow the children to dramatize the story. The additions of a box for the tub, brown paper for the mud, and a block for the scrub brush enhance the enjoyment of this activity.

✔ Compare and contrast *Strega Nona* and *The Magic Porridge Pot.* Record the comparisons.

✔ Read *The Little Old Lady Who Wasn't Afraid of Anything.* Stop reading before the conclusion of the book. Ask the children to work in pairs to predict the ending. Record their predictions on chart paper.

EXTENSION ACTIVITIES

These extension activities can be used as individual assignments.

✔ Create a reproduction of *Mrs. Wishy Washy*. The children work in pairs to illustrate one page of the text. Bind together for a class book.

✔ Children create self-portraits from colored paper and collage materials. Make a large paper shoe, staple it to a bulletin board and attach the self-portraits. Include the text for *The Old Woman in the Shoe* (see Oral Language Development).

✔ After reading *Strega Nona*, dye pasta. Provide a variety of pasta shapes. Each child places some pasta in a clear plastic resealable bag with 1 tbsp. of rubbing alcohol and food coloring of choice. By kneading the bag, the pasta will assume the chosen color. Pour colored pasta on newspaper to dry. This will dry in approximately 15 minutes. Use the colored pasta to create pasta collages.

MATH ACTIVITIES

✔ Create individual graphs using a variety of dried pasta.

✔ Sort and classify dried pasta.

✔ Read and act out "This Old Man" (traditional song).

BOOKLIST

Elizabeth and Larry by Marilyn Sadler (Simon and Schuster, 1990)

The Little Old Lady Who Wasn't Afraid of Anything by Linda Williams (Crowell, 1986)

The Magic Porridge Pot by Paul Galdone (Houghton Mifflin, 1979)

Mrs. Wishy Washy by Joy Cowley (The Wright Group, 1980)

Strega Nona by Tomie dePaola (Simon and Schuster, 1975)

The Teeny Tiny Woman by Paul Galdone (Clarion, 1984)

There Was an Old Lady Who Swallowed a Fly by Pam Adams (Child's Play Ltd., 1973)

Spring

The children's fascination with planting seeds and watching them "grow" into plants or flowers was the incentive for this unit. It is now a kindergarten "traditional" that continues to be popular with children year after year.

AREA DESIGN

Dramatic Play

Flower Shop

GENERAL PROPS
- Plastic or silk flowers
- Cash register
- Aprons
- Pots and planters
- Plastic gardening tools
- Florist flower boxes
- Ribbon and tissue paper
- Plastic watering can

PROPS TO ENCOURAGE LITERACY
- Seed catalogs
- Seed packets
- Order pad
- Florist greeting cards
- Books about flowers and flower arranging
- Pictures of plants, flowers, spring (for walls)

Sensory Table

- Dirt
- Gardening gloves
- Plastic gardening tools
- Sticks with seed packets attached

Art

- Variety of seeds
- Tissue paper and green paper strips
- Seed or flower catalogs
- Flower templates
- Pipe cleaners

Listening Center

- Theme-appropriate cassette tape and book: *The Carrot Seed*

Science Center

- Variety of seeds
- Corresponding seed packets
- Sorting tray or tray divided into sections
- Tweezers for sorting
- Magnifying glass
- Paper and pencils for recording observations
- Books about seeds and plants

Writing Center

- Pencils with flower toppers
- Blank books with flowers on the cover
- Seed packets labeled with name of item in large print
- Sentence strip attached to center: My favorite flower is_____.
- Flower word cards to complete sentence above

Block Center

- Plastic gardening tools
- Plastic fruits and vegetables
- Gardening hats and gloves
- Craft sticks, blank paper and pencils, seed catalogs for creating garden signs

Game Table

Flower Collection Game

Create the flower game board by gluing 1-inch squares of paper in a circle on a piece of poster board. Glue a flower picture from a seed catalog on various squares. Create individual flowers for the players to collect by gluing a paper flower shape on a wooden craft stick. Place this flower collection in a small flower pot in the middle of the game board circle.

Provide a die and two markers. The players toss the die and move the marker along the path. When the player lands on a flower picture, he or she may collect a paper flower. The winner is the player with the most flowers.

GROUP TIME ACTIVITIES

These activities involve the whole class.

Oral Language Development

INTERACTIVE CHARTS

The Planting Song

I dig, dig, dig.
I plant some seeds.
I rake, rake, rake.
I pull some weeds.
I watch and wait,
And soon I know:
My _____ sprouts,
My _____ grows.

Create matching pairs of flower, fruit, or vegetable cards to fill in the blank spaces.

Planting a Rainbow

Mom and _____ plant a rainbow.
It will soon be spring, you know.
They will plant _____ seeds
And watch the rainbow grow!

Create word cards for the blank spaces.
1: (Child's name)
2: (Name of a flower, fruit, or vegetable)

Flowers

The sun will shine.
The rain will fall.
And _____ flowers
Will grow up tall.

Create word cards of color words to fill in the blank space in the text.

SONGS/POEMS/FINGERPLAYS

The Seed

Dig a little hole,
Plant a little seed,
Pour a little water,
Pull a little weed.
Chase a little bug,
Heigh-ho there he goes.
Give a little sunshine,
Let it grow, grow, grow.

Allow the children to act out each
line of the poem.

Little Seed

I plant a little seed
In the dark, dark ground.
Out comes the yellow sun, big and
round,
Down comes the cool rain, soft
and slow,
Up come the little seed—
grow, grow, grow.

How Does Your Garden Grow?

Corn stalks grow high,
way up in the sky.
Watermelons are round
and grow on the ground,
But under the ground,
where no one can see,
Grow potatoes, and onions,
and carrots. All three.

Allow the children to act out each
line of the poem.

FLANNEL BOARD STORY

Create felt story characters for
The Carrot Seed.

Literacy Development

✔ Brainstorm a list of what children know about spring.

✔ After reading *Growing Vegetable
Soup* create a list of how to
grow a seed.

✔ After reading *Over in the
Meadow* with the children create a list of the animal characters from the story. Use the list
to create name tags and allow
the children to dramatize the
story.

✔ Innovate flower names for "The
Planting Song" on page 71.

✔ After reading *The Very
Hungry Caterpillar* cover the
names of the days of the
week. Ask children to predict
the names of the day. Write
their predictions on the
paper. Compare their predictions with the printed text.

✔ Compare and contrast *The Carrot Seed* and *Growing Vegetable Soup*. Record students' comparisons.

✔ Read *Jack and the Beanstalk*. With the children, create two lists: 1) What did Jack do that you liked? 2) What did Jack do that you did not like?

✔ Provide materials to plant seeds. Record the sequence of events as the children perform the planting. Record predictions as to what type of seed will sprout first. The seeds can be planted in the Sensory Table.

✔ Grow seeds in a variety of formats: in dirt, in a moist paper towel and jar, on a damp sponge, etc. Allow children to work with a classmate to predict which seed will sprout first.

✔ Brainstorm a list of spring activities with the children.

EXTENSION ACTIVITIES

These extension activities can be used as individual assignments.

✔ Create a mural of *Over in the Meadow*. Provide appropriate color paper and collage materials. The children choose a character and create it for the mural.

✔ After reading *Planting a Rainbow*, create tissue flowers. Provide children with colored tissue squares and green paper strips. To carry the flowers fold a piece of paper into a cone shape.

✔ After reading *The Carrot Seed*, provide materials for children to plant carrots.

✔ Children can create personal charts of "Flowers" on page 71. Ask children to create color word cards for the blank space.

✔ After reading *Jack and the Beanstalk*, provide materials for children to plant a bean seed. Children can draw and cut out a figure to resemble Jack. Attach this to a wooden craft stick and place by the "beanstalk."

MATH ACTIVITIES

✔ Read *Counting Wildflowers* and encourage children to illustrate the text.

✔ Graph which seed will sprout first (see Literacy Development).

✔ Create flowers with geometric shapes.

✔ Measure different flowers with a ruler or unifix cubes. Record the results.

BOOKLIST

The Carrot Seed by Ruth Krauss (Scholastic, 1945)

Counting Wildflowers by Bruce McMillan (Lothrop, 1988)

From Seed to Plant by Gail Gibbons (Holiday House, 1991)

A Garden Alphabet by Isabel Wilmer (Dutton's, 1991)

Growing Vegetable Soup by Lois Ehlert (Harcourt Brace Jovanovich, 1987)

Jack and the Beanstalk by Matt Faulkner (Scholastic, 1965)

Over in the Meadow by Ezra Jack Keats (Scholastic, 1971)

Planting a Rainbow by Lois Ehlert (Harcourt Brace Jovanovich, 1988)

Spring by Fiona Pragoff (Alladin Books, 1993)

The Very Hungry Caterpillar by Eric Carle (Scholastic, 1987)

Thanksgiving

This unit provides rich opportunities for comparing current and traditional family celebrations, and introduces the children to cultural awareness and historical time lines. I like to introduce patterning activities during this unit.

AREA DESIGN

Dramatic Play

Indian Village

GENERAL PROPS
- Tepee created from brown paper
- Wood for fire circle
- Leather strips
- Moccasins
- Feathers
- Large tubs of dirt, corn seeds, sticks to replicate planting
- Paper fish, nets, drying rack
- Clay
- Beads, string
- Basket of gourds, dried corn

PROPS TO ENCOURAGE LITERACY
- Books describing Indian writing
- Brown paper, watercolor paint to recreate Indian picture writing

Art Center

- Feathers
- Dried beans, seeds
- Indian corn kernels
- Variety of small geometric shapes for pattern designs

Listening Center

Theme-appropriate cassette tape and book: *Buried Secrets*

Writing Center

- Sentence strip: What will you eat for Thanksgiving dinner?
- Thanksgiving food word cards
- Examples of Indian picture writing
- Thanksgiving word bank (see Literacy Development)

Block Center

- Globe
- Mayflower sign
- White bed sheet
- Compass
- Binoculars

Children can recreate the *Mayflower's* crossing to America.

Game Table

Indian Stone Game
Use three craft sticks to recreate designs (see photo below). Provide a basket of small stones and scoring card. As children toss the sticks, they use the scoring card to determine the number of stones to collect.

Sensory Table

Mayflower Floating Experiments

- Water
- Two large rocks placed on opposite sides of the Sensory Table. (label one rock ENGLAND, the other AMERICA)
- Variety of materials for children to create boats: Styrofoam™ cups, paper tubes, tin foil, wood pieces, etc.

Science Center

- Indian corn
- Empty corn cobs
- Corn kernels
- Trays for sorting
- Magnifying glass
- Tweezers for kernel sorting

Easel

- Brown paper
- Paint with sticks for brushes

Children can recreate Indian-style art.

GROUP TIME ACTIVITIES

These activities involve the whole class.

Oral Language Development

INTERACTIVE CHARTS

Thanksgiving Day
(To the tune: "The Farmer in the Dell")

The _____ ran away
Before Thanksgiving Day.
He said "They'll make
a _____ of me,
If I decide to stay."

Create pairs of word cards to fill in the blanks: turkey; roast; pumpkin; pie; cranberry sauce; bread; stuffing.

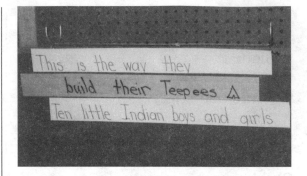

Ten Little Indian Boys and Girls

This is the way they_____
Ten little Indian boys and girls.

Children can create phrases of things Indian children might do.

I Can Hardly Wait

____ more days till Thanksgiving.
____ more days till Thanksgiving.
____ more days till Thanksgiving.
And I can hardly wait!

We will eat some _____.
We will eat some _____.
We will eat some _____.
And I can hardly wait!

POEMS/ SONGS/
FINGERPLAYS

Guess What Day?

There's a turkey in the oven,
Pumpkin pie to eat.
Stuffing, chestnuts, cranberries,
It is a special treat.

With families all together,
Their happy faces bright.
Can you guess what day this is?
Thanksgiving Day—that's right!

Hungry Birds

I gather up the crumbs and scraps,
When everyone is through.
And then I give the hungry birds
A nice Thanksgiving, too!

Funny Turkey

The turkey is a funny bird.
His head goes wobble, wobble,
And all he says is just one word—
Gobble, gobble, gobble.

FLANNEL BOARD STORY

Create felt pieces to retell *The Thanksgiving Story*.

Literacy Development

With the children, brainstorm a list of what the children know about pilgrims, Native Americans, and the first Thanksgiving. Record items on chart paper.

✔ Read *Buried Secrets*. Create a graph comparing various Indian tribes. Categories might include the name of the tribe, type of homes, food sources, etc.

✔ List the names of various Indian tribes. With the children, clap the syllables. Group the tribe names into syllable groups, those containing one syllable, two syllables, etc.

✔ Read *Sarah Morton's Day* and *Samuel Eaton's Day*. Create a Venn diagram listing daily responsibilities of a girl and a boy pilgrim. Then create a section listing duties shared by both children.

✔ Dramatize the *Mayflower* crossing. Use blocks to create the parameters of the ship. Ask the children to solve some problems that occurred on the *Mayflower*: sick pilgrims, storms, lack of drinking water, etc.

✔ With the children, create a Thanksgiving word bank. Place these words in the Writing Center for independent use.

✔ Have the children create and record new verses for *We Can Hardly Wait*.

✔ Read *The Thanksgiving Story*. Discuss family traditions and individual responsibilities for Thanksgiving Day.

EXTENSION ACTIVITY

This extension activity can be used as an individual assignment.

✔ Create Plymouth Colony: Using a long table for the display, each child creates the following items to reproduce Plymouth Colony.

• Pilgrim Houses: Cover small milk cartons with paper. Cut yellow paper into strips for the roof to simulate the straw roofs.

• Wampanog Indian Wigwams: Cover inverted paper bowls with torn pieces of a brown paper bag.

• Fall Garden: Roll and tape yellow paper into a tube. Make small cuts at the top to replicate corn husks. Roll orange Play-Doh™ into balls. Insert a whole clove into the top to replicate pumpkins. Add green yarn or ribbon for the vines.

• Magnificent Mayflower: The children paint several boxes with brown paint. Attach the boxes to replicate the *Mayflower*. Attach drinking straws and paper for the sails and masts.

MATH ACTIVITIES

✔ Explore patterning: Create Indian headbands, vests or necklaces using patterns.

✔ Read *1 2 3 Thanksgiving*. With the children create an innovation of the text. Children work cooperatively to illustrate each page.

✔ Ask: Where do you go for Thanksgiving? Graph students' choices.

✔ Read *The Popcorn Book*. Estimate the number of popcorn kernels in a cup. Check the estimations by counting kernels in groups of tens.

COOKING ACTIVITIES

✔ Make butter: Put cream in a small glass jar. Label the jar "Cream" with self-sticking paper. Each child takes a turn shaking the jar. Remove the "Cream" label and replace it with the label "Butter." Sample the butter on crackers.

✔ Make cranberry bread or relish.

BOOKLIST

1 2 3 Thanksgiving by W. Nikola-Lisa (Albert Whitman, 1991)

Buried Secrets by Jane Ann Thomas (Nystrom, 1990)

The First Thanksgiving Feast by Joan Anderson (Clarion, 1984)

Oh, What a Thanksgiving! by Steven Kroll (Scholastic, 1988)

The Popcorn Book by Tomie dePaola (Scholastic, 1978)

Samuel Eaton's Day by Kate Waters (Scholastic, 1993)

Sarah Morton's Day by Kate Waters (Scholastic, 1989)

The Story of the First Thanksgiving by Elaine Raphael and Don Bolognese (Scholastic, 1991)

The Thanksgiving Story by Alice Dalgliesh (Scholastic, 1990)

A Turkey for Thanksgiving by Eve Bunting (Scholastic, 1991)

Transportation

I use this unit at the end of September or early October when we review bus safety and procedures for crossing the street. This unit has a focus on fire safety. One year after touring the neighborhood firehouse, two students said to me, "Thank you for teaching us about trucks!" Based on that comment, one can guess how popular this unit is with the children!

AREA DESIGN

Dramatic Play

Fire Station

GENERAL PROPS
- Telephone
- Fire hats and coats
- Gloves
- Refrigerator box painted red
- Buckets
- Hose

PROPS TO ENCOURAGE LITERACY
- Telephone book
- Map of area
- Paper and pencils
- Clipboards for fire reports
- Books about firefighters
- Pegboard with clipboard reading: Please write your fire report.

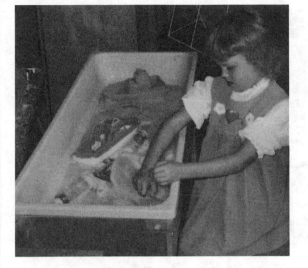

Sensory Table

- Water, water pumps
- Plastic boats

Art Center

- Catalogs from local car dealers
- Vehicle templates
- Toothpicks, paper circles for creating vehicles
- Geometric paper shapes

Listening Center

- Theme-appropriate cassette tape and book: *Who Sank the Boat?*

Science Center

- Assortment of unit blocks
- Toy cars, trucks

Children can create inclines and experiment with degrees of speed.

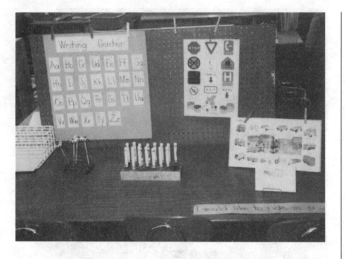

Writing Center

- Pencils with plastic cars glued to their tops
- Blank books with vehicles on the covers
- Sentence strip reading: I like to ride in a _____.
- Labeled picture cards of vehicles
- Examples of street signs: stop sign, traffic light, etc.

Game Table

- Two grids drawn on card stock (divide each paper into 12 squares)
- Basket of plastic vehicles
- Spinner or die

Children can invent their own games using these items.

Block Center

- Variety of vehicles
- Wooden traffic signs
- Books about traffic signs: *I Can Read Symbols*
- Blank cards, pencils, tape for creating traffic signs

GROUP TIME ACTIVITIES

These activities involve the whole class.

FLANNEL BOARD STORY

Create felt pieces to retell *Who Sank the Boat?*

Oral Language Development

INTERACTIVE CHARTS

Hurry Hurry

Hurry hurry _____.
Hurry hurry _____.
Hurry hurry _____.
Ding, ding, ding, ding, ding!

Create three sets of matching word cards for the blank spaces. Suggestions include: drive the firetruck, climb the ladder, squirt the water.

The Railroad Track

A _____ was on a railroad track
Its heart was all a-flutter.
Along came a choo-choo train
Toot, toot, _____.

Create word card pairs of food items that change form, such as: peanut/peanut butter, cracker/crumbs, tomato/catsup. Children fill in the blank spaces in the chart with the correct pairs in the correct order.

POEMS/SONGS/ FINGERPLAYS

If I Had

If I had a _____
Zoom, zoom, zoom.
I would go to Mexico
Wave my hands and off I'd go.
If I had a _____
Zoom, zoom, zoom.

Children select vehicle names for blank spaces.

Here Is the Choo Choo

Here is the choo choo on the track.
Now it choo choos forward,
Now it choo choos back.
Now the bell is ringing,
Ding, ding, ding, ding, ding.
Hurry up and take a seat
The train is about to go!

Motions can be added to dramatize the poem. Speed up the tempo with each repetition to simulate a train.

Literacy Development

✔ Enclose a fireman's hat, gloves and the book *Fire, Fire* in a box. Encourage the children to guess the contents by asking "Yes" or "No" questions. This activity can serve as the introduction to the theme.

✔ Encourage children to dramatize each vehicle in the book *To Town*.

✔ After reading *To Town*, cover the vehicle names. Encourage the children to contribute the initial, middle, and ending sounds of the covered word.

✔ After reading *I Can Read Symbols*, children can create signs for the classroom and playground.

✔ Read *The Bus Ride*. Write the initial consonant of a character on a sentence strip. Allow the children to guess the character based on the initial letter. Use these character cards to dramatize the story.

✔ Compare and contrast *The Bus Ride* and *The Bus Stop*. Record the similarities and differences.

✔ With the children, create word cards for the poem "If I Had" on this page.

✔ Write a thank-you letter to the fire station (see Field Trips).

EXTENSION ACTIVITIES

These activities can be used as individual assignments.

✔ Allow the children to dip the wheels of a toy car in paint and "drive" it on a dark colored piece of paper to create a design.

✔ Reproduce and give each child the repetitive sentence from *The Bus Ride*: The _____ got on the bus. Encourage children to add a person's name in the blank space and illustrate the sentence. Gather all illustrated sentences and create a class book.

✔ Children create collages by cutting pictures of vehicles from magazines.

MATH ACTIVITIES

✔ Read *Changes, Changes*. Children can work in pairs and create vehicles using blocks. Provide paper shapes so that children can recreate their block vehicles.

✔ Graph the different ways the children get to school: bus, walk, car, etc.

FIELD TRIPS

✔ Visit the local fire station.

✔ Visit a local car dealership.

BOOKLIST

The Bus Ride by (Scott Foresman, 1976)

The Bus Stop by Nancy Hellen (Orchard Books, 1988)

Changes, Changes by Pat Hutchins (MacMillan, 1971)

Dan the Flying Man by Joy Cowley (The Wright Group, 1983)

Fire Engines by Anne Rockwell (The Trumpet Club, 1986)

Fire! Fire! by Gail Gibbons (Crowell, 1984)

I Read Signs by Tana Hoban (Greenwllow, 1971)

This Is the Way We Go to School by Edith Baer (Scholastic, 1990)

To Town by Joy Cowley (The Wright Group, 1983)

Wheels by Venice Shone (Scholastic, 1990)

The Wheels on the Bus by Raffi Songs to Read (Crown, 1988)

Who Sank the Boat? by Pamela Allen (Coward-McCann, 1982)

Valentine's Day

This unit was developed using the excitement of Valentine's Day celebrations to encourage the children to engage in meaningful and relevant writing activities. Children enjoy writing and mailing letters to their families. Our local post office personnel is helpful and very patient while the children choose stamps for their letters. Be sure to have plenty of envelopes available during this unit!

AREA DESIGN

Dramatic Play

Post Office

GENERAL PROPS
- Cash register
- Telephone
- Mail carrier hats, mail bags
- Sorting boxes, wrapped boxes
- Mail box
- Scale

PROPS TO ENCOURAGE LITERACY
- Junk mail
- Rubber stamps
- Used postage stamps
- Price list for stamps and packages
- Sign denoting mail pickup schedule
- Posters from local post office
- Paper, pencils, envelopes
- Name cards of class members

Writing Center

- Pencils with heart toppers
- Blank books with hearts glued to the cover
- Name cards of class members
- Variety of stationery, note cards
- Candy hearts and paper hearts (children can copy message on to a paper heart before eating candy)
- Letter-writing word bank: word cards with helpful words for writing letters (Dear, love, date, etc.)

Art Center

- Heart templates
- Red and pink construction paper
- Paper doilies
- Tissue squares
- Envelopes

Listening Center

- Theme-appropriate cassette tape and book: *A Letter to Amy*

Packages

Science Center

- Scale
- Variety of items for weighing
- Sentence strip that reads:
  "_____ is heavier than
  _____." " _____ is lighter
  than _____."
- Index cards and pencils for
  completing sentences.

Game Table

- Two small mailboxes
- Basket of Valentine cards
- Spinner or die

Children use materials to create
rules to play the game. This can
be correlated with *Millions of
Valentines*.

GROUP TIME ACTIVITIES

These activities involve the whole
class.

Oral Language Development

INTERACTIVE CHARTS

Little Red Box

I wish I had a little red box
to put that _____ in.
I'd take _____ out
and kiss, kiss, kiss,
And put _____ back in again.

Create an individual name card
for each class member for the first
blank space in the poem. Create
two sets of cards for the remain-
ing spaces: two cards labeled
"him" and two cards labeled "her."

I Love Somebody
(To the tune: "Skip to My Lou")

I love somebody, yes, I do.
I love somebody, _____ its you.
I love somebody, yes, I do.
I love _____.

Create a set of name cards to fill
in the blank spaces.

SONGS/POEMS/FINGERPLAYS

The Postman

The postman brings a valentine,
A valentine, a valentine.
The postman brings a valentine
It says that I love _____.

Red Valentines

One red valentine,
Two red valentines,
Three red valentines,
Four.
We'll cut and cut,
And paste and paste,
And then make many
more.

Address Song
(To the tune: "The
Muffin Man")

Oh, do you know
_____

who lives on
_____?

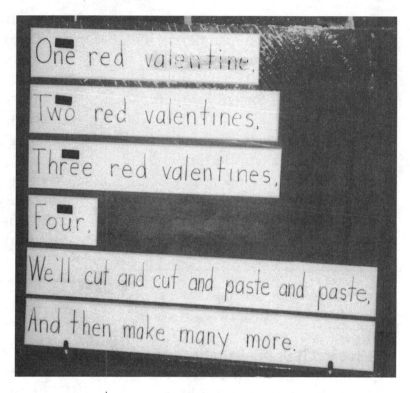

Fill in blank spaces with child's
name and address.

Literacy Development

✔ With the children, brainstorm a
   list of necessary items to create
   a dramatic-play post office.
   Read *The Mail and How It
   Moves* and revise the list.

✔ With the children, create a word
   bank of appropriate valentine
   greetings. Add these to the
   Writing Center.

✔ Compare and contrast *The Jolly
   Postman* and *The Postman.*

✔ Read *A Letter to Amy.* Stop
   reading before the end of the
   book. Encourage the children to
   solve the story's problem.
   Finish the book. Allow children
   to alter or confirm their solu-
   tions.

✔ Display and discuss may different types of mail: a personal
   letter, a postcard, an advertise-
   ment, a bill, etc. Read *The Jolly
   Postman.*

✔ With the children create a story
   map, listing the route of *The
   Jolly Postman.*

✔ With the children, write a letter
   to another classroom.

✔ Create a list of places in the community that a mail carrier would encounter on the mail route. *Rosie's Walk* could provide a model for this activity.

✔ Visit a local post office and write a thank-you letter.

EXTENSION ACTIVITIES

These activities can be used as individual assignments.

✔ Give each child a photocopy of the song "Little Red Box." Provide name cards of class members so children can create their own word cards for the blank spaces.

✔ Children can illustrate a favorite memory from the visit to the post office.

✔ With adult assistance, each child can write a letter to a family member. These can be mailed during the post office visit.

MATH ACTIVITIES

✔ Children can graph candy conversation hearts by color or message.

✔ Give each child a photocopy of the song "Red Valentines" on page 91. Leave a blank in place of the word "many" in the text. Children can cut out heart shapes, glue them to the chart, and write in the corresponding number.

✔ Create a graph predicting how many days it will take for the individual letters to reach their destinations.

BOOKLIST

The Jolly Postman by Janet Ahlberg and Allan Ahlberg (Little, Brown, 1986)

A Letter to Amy by Ezra Jack Keats (Harper and Row, 1968)

Mail and How It Moves by Gail Gibbons (Trumpet Club, 1981)

The Missing Tarts by B.G. Hennessey (Scholastic, 1991)

One Zillion Valentines by Frank Modell (Trumpet Club, 1981)

The Post Office Book by Gail Gibbons (Harper Collins, 1982)

Thank You Santa by Margaret Wila (Scholastic, 1991)

Weather

This unit was created upon dis-covering the popularity of the book *It Looked Like Spilt Milk* with the children. Since that time many wonderful books about weather have been added to this unit. I like to do this unit as a lead-in to the Spring unit. It is a smooth transition and the curriculum maintains its focus for the children.

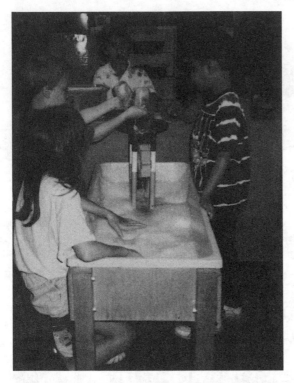

AREA DESIGN

Sensory Table

- Water
- Waterwheels
- Plastic cups

Art Center

- Cotton balls
- Small pieces of tin foil
- White packing material
- Blue or black paper
- Yellow paper circles and triangles to create a sun shape

Listening Center

Theme-appropriate cassette tape and book: *It Looked Like Spilt Milk*

Writing Center

- Blank books made from blue construction paper (a rainbow or cloud sticker can be placed on the cover)
- Sentence strip with the phrase from *It Looked Like Spilt Milk*: "Sometimes it looked like a _____."
- A copy of *It Looked Like Spilt Milk*
- Picture cards of cloud shapes (refer to *It Looked Like Spilt Milk* for suggestions)

Science Center

- Pinwheels
- Bicycle pump and balloons

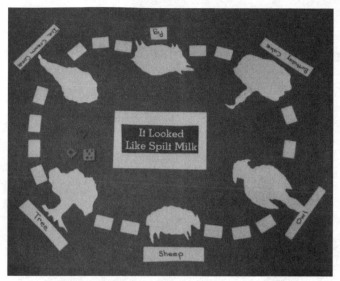

Game Table

Cloud Game

Using blue poster board and white paper squares, create a path game. Place a cloud shape between every two or three squares. Provide two markers, a die, and a basket of cotton balls for keeping score. This game can be made in a circle shape so that the players determine the beginning, the end, and how to keep score. This can be correlated with *It Looked Like Spilt Milk*. Refer to this book for cloud shape suggestions.

Clay Table

- Blue Play-Doh™
- Small rolling pins
- Small plastic knives.
- Books about Clouds

Children can cut the Play-Doh™ to resemble clouds.

Easel

- Blue paper
- White paint

GROUP TIME ACTIVITIES

These activities involve the whole class.

Oral Language Development

INTERACTIVE CHARTS

Clouds

I thought I saw a _____ way up in the sky.
I thought I saw so many things as clouds went drifting by.

Create word cards so children can fill in the blank space in the poem. Suggestions: a pig, a horse, and an ice cream cone.

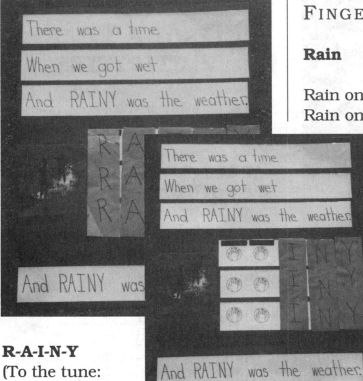

R-A-I-N-Y
(To the tune: "Bingo")

There was a time when we got wet,
And RAINY was the weather.
R-A-I-N-Y
R-A-I-N-Y
R-A-I-N-Y
and RAINY was the weather.

Create letter strips for the portion of the song where the word "rainy" is spelled out, and hang them on the chart. As the children sing the song, they remove each strip in turn,

revealing a picture of clapping hands, which reminds them to clap instead of sing. See photos.

SONGS/POEMS/FINGERPLAYS

Rain

Rain on the rooftops,
Rain on the trees.
Rain on the green grass,
But not on me!

Clouds

Floating pictures in the sky,
Upon a cloud I'd like to fly.
And see the world from way up high
Come and ride a cloud with me.

The Clouds

The clouds are dark and angry
They must be sad, it's true.
For when a cloud is crying
The rain is falling through.

My Umbrella

Pitter patter raindrops
Falling from the sky,
Here is my umbrella
To keep me safe and dry.

Rain, Rain
(To the tune: "Row Row, Row Your Boat")

Rain, rain, falling down
Landing all around.
What a lovely sound you make
Splashing on the ground.

FLANNEL BOARD STORY

Cut shapes from white felt to replicate the cloud shapes in *It Looked Like Spilt Milk*.

Literacy Development

✔ Read *It Looked Like Spilt Milk*. Brainstorm a list of what the children know about clouds.

✔ With the children, innovate new verses for "Clouds" on page 96.

✔ Read *The Cloud Book*. After the children have looked out the windows and observed the sky, create a list of different cloud shapes or types of clouds based on their observations.

✔ Read *One Cold Wet Night* and create a list of characters from the story. Use this list to create individual name tags. Distribute the name tags to children and dramatize the story. Include the repeated phrase "SKIDDLE-DEE-DOO", for a child to hold up as it occurs in the story.

✔ Read *Who Is Tapping at My Window?* Stop reading before the last page and make predictions. Finish the story and allow the children to alter or confirm their predictions.

✔ After the children are familiar with the song "R-A-I-N-Y" on page 96, create multiple sets of letter cards, using the letters R, A, I, N, and Y. Distribute one letter card to each child. As that letter is used in the song, the children holding the appropriate letter cards may hold it in the air.

✔ Read *A Rainbow of My Own*. Children can work in pairs to predict how a rainbow is created. Children may record their predictions on paper and share them with the whole group.

EXTENSION ACTIVITIES

These extension activities can be used as individual assignments.

✔ Create a blow-painting picture. Drop a spoonful of white paint on to blue paper. With a straw, the child blows air above the paint, until the desired shape is achieved. Duplicate the sentence from *It Looked Like Spilt Milk*: Sometimes it looked like a _____. Each child may fill in the blank space with a word to describe his or her painting.

✔ Create a storm mural. Children can create a storm picture using a large piece of black bulletin-board paper as the background and collage materials for the storm. Items might include: tin foil for raindrops, yellow yarn for lightning, white, gray, and blue tissue for clouds, white Styrofoam™ packing materials for wind and rain.

✔ Children can create and color a house to replicate their own home. Record each child's dictation of enjoyable rainy day activities on the inside of the house. This can be attached to the bottom of the storm mural.

✔ Create windsocks: The children staple a strip of paper at the ends to create a circle. Glue long strips of crepe paper to the circle. These can be suspended from the classroom ceiling with string so that they move when the windows are open.

✔ Create a reproduction of *Rain*. Each child illustrates a page using appropriate collage materials. This can be bound together for a class book.

✔ After reading *A Rainbow of My Own* and discussing rainbows (see Literacy Development), children may create rainbow marble paintings. Place a piece of blue paper in a tray. Apply small spoonfuls of paint, one for each color of the rainbow, in various places on the paper. Place a marble on the tray. Children tilt the tray, allowing the marble to roll through the paint. This creates a rainbow effect.

MATH ACTIVITIES

✔ Provide prisms for the children to explore during free time. At the end of the week, create a graph titled "Did You See a Rainbow with the Prism?" The children record their names under YES or NO.

✔ Brainstorm a list of storms: tornado, thunder, blizzard, etc. Each child illustrates one of the storms. Sort and classify the pictures. This can lead to a discussion of weather safety.

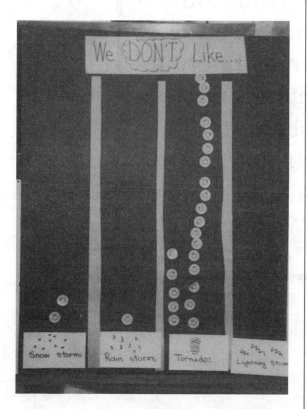

BOOKLIST

The Cloud Book by Tomie dePaola (Holiday House, 1975)

Dreams by Peter Spier (Doubleday, 1986)

It Looked Like Spilt Milk by Charles G. Shaw (Harper and Row, 1947)

One Cold Wet Night by June Melser and Joy Cowley (The Wright Group, 1980)

Rain by Robert Kalan (Mulberry, 1978)

Rain by Peter Spier (Doubleday, 1982)

A Rainbow of My Own by Don Freeman (Viking, 1966)

Sun Up, Sun Down by Gail Gibbons (Harcourt Brace Jovanovich, 1983)

Who Is Tapping at My Window? by A. G. Deming (Dutton, 1988)

Winter

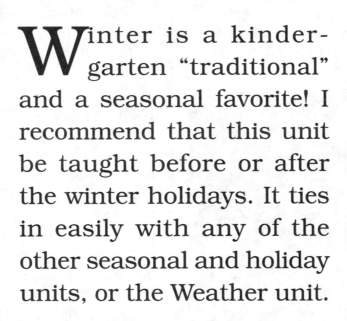

Winter is a kinder-garten "traditional" and a seasonal favorite! I recommend that this unit be taught before or after the winter holidays. It ties in easily with any of the other seasonal and holiday units, or the Weather unit.

AREA DESIGN

Sensory Table

- Bird seed
- Funnels
- Plastic scoops

or

- Snow
- Mittens
- Colored water in squeeze bottles
- Plastic shovels

Writing Center

- Labeled picture cards of winter clothing from *The Jacket I Wear in the Snow*
- Blank books with a snowman on the cover
- Pencils with snowmen on the tops

Art Center

- Cotton balls
- Styrofoam packing material
- Blue construction paper
- Snowmen templates
- Variety of circle templates for creating snowmen

Listening Center

Theme-appropriate cassette tape and book: *The Snowy Day*

Science Center

- Variety of pinecones
- Pine tree branch
- Magnifying glasses
- Paper and pencils to record observations

Block Center

- Large container of white Styrofoam™ packing material
- Shovels

Easel

- Blue paper
- White paint

Game Table

Board game based on *The Snowy Day*.

GROUP TIME ACTIVITIES

These activities involve the whole class.

Oral Language Development

INTERACTIVE CHART

Five Little Snowmen

_____ little snowmen standing in a row.
Each with a hat and a big red bow.

Have the students create number cards for the blank space.

Five Snowmen

_____ little snowmen all made of snow,
_____ little snowmen standing in a row,
Out came the sun and stayed all day.
And one little snowman melted away.

Create two sets of cards numbered five through one. Children change the cards as they say the rhyme. Place five detachable snowmen at the bottom of the chart. The children remove a snowman each time one "melts."

POEMS/SONGS/
FINGERPLAYS

One Little Snowman
(To the tune: "Ten Little Indians")

One little, two little, three little snowmen,
four little, five little, six little snowmen,
seven little, eight little, nine little snowmen,
ten little snowmen bright.

A Chubby Little Snowman
(To the tune: "Sing a Song of Sixpence")

A chubby little snowman
Had a carrot nose.
Along came a bunny
And what do you suppose?
That hungry little bunny,
Looking for some lunch,
Ate that little snowman's nose,
Nibble, nibble, crunch.

It Looked Like

It looked like balls of cotton,
It looked like cookie dough.
It looked like my white blanket,
It was snow, snow, snow.

Shiver and Quiver
(To the tune: "When You're Happy and You Know It")

When it's cold, you shiver and quiver, BRRRRRR.
When it's cold, you shiver and quiver, BRRRRRR.
Your hands feel just like ice.
So you rub them once or twice.
When it's cold you shiver and quiver, BRRRRRR.

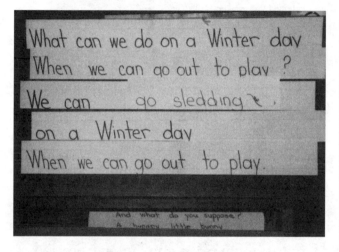

Winter Day
(To the tune: "Mulberry Bush")

What can we do on a winter day
When we can go out to play?
We can _____
on a winter day
When you can go out and play.

Create word cards of winter activities for the blank.

FLANNEL BOARD STORY

Create felt pieces to retell *A Snowy Day*.

Literacy Development

✔ Create an attribute box of winter clothing. Encourage the children to ask "Yes" or "No" questions. Record all correct answers and tape them to the outside of the box. Encourage the children to guess the contents based on the recorded guesses. Reveal the contents, then read *The Jacket I Wear in the Snow*.

✔ With the children, brainstorm a list of what they know about winter. Record their comments.

✔ Brainstorm a list of snowy day activities. Record the activities and use this list to complete the song "A Winter Day" on this page. Read *The Snowy Day* and alter the list if necessary.

✔ Read *The Mitten* and encourage the children to recall the characters. Record each character's name on a sentence strip. Ask children to identify the characters based on the initial consonants.

✔ Dramatize *The Mitten*.

✔ Compare and contrast *The Mitten* and *The Woodcutter's Mitten*.

✔ Use the contents of the attribute box to dramatize *The Jacket I Wear in the Snow*.

✔ Using the contents of the attribute box, ask students to match appropriate word cards to the items.

✔ Map the events in *Katie and the Big Snow*.

✔ Read *Sadie and the Snowman*. Record estimates for the amount of time it would take snow or an ice cube to melt in the classroom. Conduct an experiment to test predictions.

✔ Read *Katie and the Big Snow*. Give some children a sentence strip with the repetitive refrain: "Follow me." The children can hold this up in the air as the refrain occurs in the story.

EXTENSION ACTIVITIES

These activities can be used as individual assignments.

✔ *Our Snowy Day* Language-Experience Book: Each child creates a picture of a favorite snowy day activity. Collage materials can be used such as blue paper, white tissue, Styrofoam™ packing material, etc. Record each child's narrative and attach to the picture for the text. Bind for a class book.

✔ Personal chart of "Winter Day": Photocopy the lyrics to the song. Have each child create their own word cards for the blank space.

✔ Soap snowmen: Mix white laundry soap flakes and water until it is a clay-like consistency. Children use this to roll balls and create small snowmen. Decorate with colored popcorn, toothpicks, yarn, etc. Attach a copy of the song *A Chubby Little Snowman*.

✔ The Mitten Mural: Each child paints a favorite character from *The Mitten*. Attach the characters to a large mitten shape cut from white bulletin board paper.

✔ Geopolis model: Transform a table into Geopolis. Children decorate pint-size milk cartons with paper to resemble buildings in the story. Children glue lots of cotton balls on to paper, covering the table. Encourage the children to create signs for the different buildings. A small toy bulldozer completes the scene.

MATH ACTIVITIES

✔ Dramatize *Five Little Snowmen.*

✔ Create individual number books of *Five Little Snowmen.* Reproduce the text and have the children illustrate and sequence the pages to form a book.

✔ Graph favorite winter activities.

COOKING ACTIVITY

✔ Pinecone Bird Feeders: Children cover a pinecone with peanut butter, roll in birdseed, and tie a piece of yarn to the top. Send home in a plastic sandwich bag.

BOOKLIST

The First Snowfall by Anne Harlow and Harlow Rockwell (MacMillan, 1987)

Happy Winter by Karen Gundersheimer (Harper and Row, 1982)

How Do You Know It's Winter by Allan Fowler (Children's Press, 1991)

The Jacket I Wear in the Snow by Shirley Neitzel (Greenwillow, 1989

Katie and the Big Snow by Virginia Lee Burton (Scholastic, 1971)

The Mitten by Jan Brett (Putnam, 1989)

Sadie and the Snowman by Allen Morgan (Scholastic, 1985)

The Snowy Day by Ezra Jack Keats (Puffin Books, 1962)

When Winter Comes by Robert Maas (Henry Holt, 1993)

Winter by Fiona Pragoff (Aladdin Books, 1992)

Zoo

This unit was designed to complement our spring field trip to the local zoo. Animals are fascinating to young children and there is a great variety of animal books to feed their fascination. If visiting a zoo is not feasible, this unit could be the basis of a Rain Forest unit.

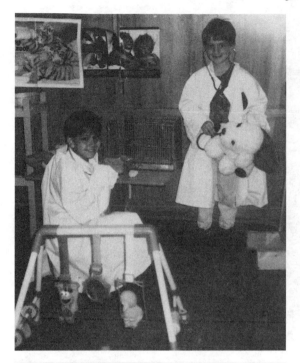

AREA DESIGN

Dramatic Play

Zoo Nursery

GENERAL PROPS
- Stuffed animals
- Empty animal cages and an aquarium
- Small fish net
- Empty pill bottles
- Cotton balls, Q-tips
- Eye droppers, stethoscope
- Lab coats
- Baby bottles, diapers
- Wash tub, sponges, towels
- Plastic fruit and vegetables
- Scale

PROPS TO ENCOURAGE LITERACY
- Zoo appointment book
- Note pads
- Feeding schedule with blank paper
- Message board
- Books related to animal care

Art Center

- Animal templates
- Feathers
- Yarn
- Craft sticks to create cages
- Scraps of fake fur or animal print fabric

Sensory Table

- Small plastic zoo animals
- Plastic or silk greenery, or trees
- Plastic strawberry baskets
- Small wooden fences

Children can create their own zoo.

Writing Center

- Picture cards of zoo animals
- Small blank books with zoo animals on cover
- Pencils with a zoo animal glued to top
- Sentence affixed to center: My favorite zoo animal is _____.
- Writing paper cut into animal shapes or with an animal border

Listening Center

Theme-appropriate book and cassette tape: *Dear Zoo*

Easel

Sponge-shaped animals for painting

Game Table

Zoo Map Game

- Zoo map board
- Two markers and die

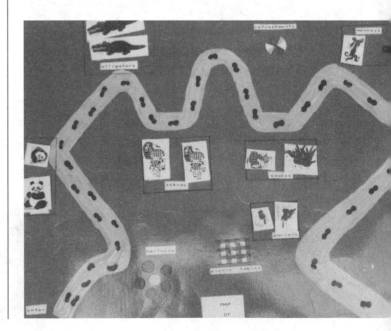

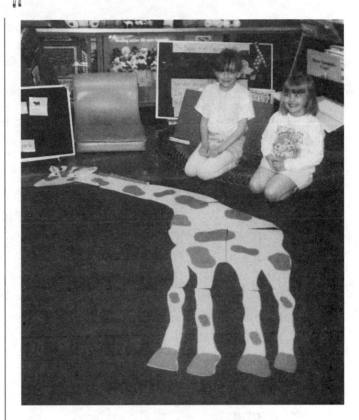

- Two zoo photo albums with an animal name listed on each page.

Create a map of a zoo on poster board. Include two animal pictures that are attached to the board with a small magnet or Velcro™ in each designated animal area. Players use a die to determine the number of steps to move their markers. As they pass an animal cage,

they collect that animal picture to add to a zoo photo album. Players match the animal to the name in the photo album. This can be self-checking by including the name of the animal on the back of the game piece. The game is finished when a player's photo album is complete. This game can be correlated with *My Camera at the Zoo*.

Science Center

- Gerbil or hamster
- Observation log: notebook for children to record observations
- Feeding schedule chart
- Books related to gerbil, hamster or other pet care

Blocks Center

- Large plastic zoo animals
- Craft sticks, index cards, tape, and pencils to create plastic zoo map (available from school supply catalogs)

GROUP TIME ACTIVITIES

These activities involve the whole class.

Oral Language Development

INTERACTIVE CHARTS

Ten Little Monkeys

Ten little monkeys
Up in a tree.
Teasing Mr. Crocodile,
Mean as can be.
Along came Mr. Crocodile
Quiet as a mouse—
Then, SNAP!

Children can change the number in the text of the poem as well as move the paper monkeys. A crocodile hand puppet can accompany this chart.

Oh, A-Hunting We Will Go

Oh, a-hunting we will go,
A-hunting we will go,
We'll catch a _____
And put him in a _____
And then we'll let him go!

Create rhyming word cards to fill in the blanks: fox/box, snake/cake, etc.

POEMS/SONGS/ FINGERPLAYS

Five Little Monkeys

Five little monkeys jumping on the bed,
One fell off and bumped his head.
Mommy called the doctor
And the doctor said,
"No more monkeys jumping on the bed!"

There's a Lion on the Prowl
(To the tune: "If You're Happy and You Know It Clap Your Hands")

There's a lion on the prowl, on the prowl (clap, clap).
There's a lion on the prowl, on the prowl (clap, clap).
There's a lion on the prowl,
He can roar and he can growl.
There's a lion on the prowl, on the prowl.

Additional verses: Snake on the wall, he can move and he can crawl; Bear in the cave, he can stand and he can wave.

One Elephant
(Traditional song)

One elephant went out to play
Upon a spider's web one day.
He had such enormous fun
That he called for another elephant to come.

FLANNEL BOARD STORY

Create a flannel board story from *The Snake that Sneezed.*

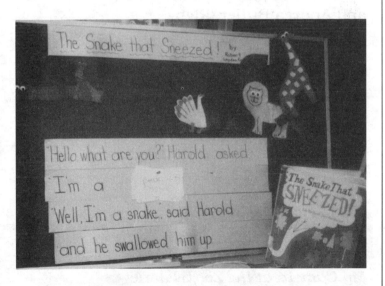

Literacy Development

✔ Children can brainstorm a list of what they know about the zoo. Read *Zoo.* Revise the list and add any additional information obtained from the book.

✔ Read *I Spy at the Zoo.* When the children have internalized the language pattern, cover the rhyming component and encourage the children to complete each sentence. Compare their predictions with the text.

✔ Brainstorm new verses for the song "There's a Lion on the Prowl" on page 110. Record new verses and encourage the children to create movements to dramatize the song.

✔ Read *My Camera at the Zoo.* Draw large squares on to a piece of bulletin board paper. Allow the children to label these areas with the names of their favorite zoo animals. Encourage the children to identify the first and last letter as you record their requests. Glue the labels to the areas on the paper.

EXTENSION ACTIVITIES

These activities can be used as individual assignments.

✔ After reading *Green Bananas,* have the children make a fruit salad.

✔ Create a class version of *A Children's Zoo*. Each child creates a favorite zoo animal and glues it to a large piece of black paper. Record each child's three descriptive words and the name of the animal. This can be bound together to create a class book.

✔ Make clay animals with Play-Doh™ and animal-shaped cookie cutters.

✔ Visit the local zoo.

MATH ACTIVITIES

✔ Graph favorite zoo animals.

✔ Dramatize "Ten Little Monkeys." Act out additional story problems, e.g., How many monkeys are left if the alligator snapped three?

✔ Read *1, 2, 3 to the Zoo*. Children create animals for a zoo train. Bind as a counting book for the classroom.

BOOKLIST

1 Hunter by Pat Hutchins (Mulberry Books, 1982)

1, 2, 3 to the Zoo by Eric Carle (Philomel, 1968)

A Children's Zoo by Tana Hoban (Mulberry Books, 1987)

Dear Zoo by Rod Campbell (Four Winds, 1982)

Elephant Buttons by Noriko Ueno (Harper and Row, 1973)

Green Bananas by Pam Neville and Andrea Butler (Rigby Heinemann, 1988)

I Spy at the Zoo by Maureen Roffey (Macmillan, 1989)

Is Your Mama a Llama? by Deborah Guarino (Scholastic, 1989)

Koala Lou by Mem Fox (Harcourt Brace Jovanovich, 1988)

My Camera at the Zoo by Janet Perry Marshall (Little, Brown, 1989)

The Snake that Sneezed by Robert Leydenfrost (Putnam, 1970)